Cristina Ferrare's
Family Entertaining

Imperia Torinesi (Nony, seated), Cristina Ferrare, Renata Ferrare

Cristina Ferrare's Family Entertaining

Celebrating the Life of the Home

ST. MARTIN'S GRIFFIN ⚜ NEW YORK

Food photography by Dick Sharpe
Styling by Marlene Brown

Recipe for Double Trouble Chocolate Bars courtesy of Marlene Brown
Pattern for title, part title, and endpapers by Micio & Company, Inc.
Photo credits: Page 6, from left, by Rusty, Francesco Scavullo, and Bill King;
page 9 by Craig Mathew; page 11 by Beverly Pomerantz;
all other photos courtesy of Cristina Ferrare

www.stmartins.com

Designed by Stephanie Tevonian

ISBN 0-312-26304-X

First published in the United States by
Golden Books, Golden Books Publishing Co., Inc.

First St. Martin's Griffin Edition: November 2000

10 9 8 7 6 5 4 3 2 1

To Nony, my grandmother. I like to think that of all her grandchildren, I am most like her. Totally irreverent and outspoken to a fault, she can tell a joke like a sailor. All her life she has loved her family, friends, cooking, and eating. As of this writing she is in the hospital, and even though she knows she has little time left, she still manages to make us laugh. That is her gift to us.

Lucky me to have had you, Nony, for all these years.

Acknowledgments

Thank you—

To God, *first and foremost, for all the blessings He has given me.*

To Tony, *for his gift of love and unwavering support, no matter what.*

To my children, *Zach, Kathryn, Alexandra, and Arianna, my reason for everything I do.*

To my mom and dad, *Renata and Tavio, for a happy childhood and a good life.*

To my stepchildren, *Anne, Denis, and Mark, my son-in-law, Patrice, and my granddaughter, Claire, for being a family.*

To Lee Bokhof, *my assistant, for her sweet nature and tireless effort in getting this book finished. I couldn't have done it without her. All her phoning, faxing, typing, and organizing helped my dream become a reality. I'm eternally grateful.*

To Woody Fraser, *longtime, dear friend and executive producer of* Home & Family. *It's been a privilege working with you. Thank you for giving me a forum to do every day what I dearly love to do.*

To my agent, Jan Miller. *This book has been in my head for years, and she helped me to move forward by believing in me and encouraging me to put it on paper. She is my girlfriend and I adore her!*

To Cassie Jones, *book editor. I need to mention how incredibly persistent and unwaveringly supportive she has been during this project. Her patience, graciousness, and kindness helped me to actually finish this book. I can't believe she didn't choke me in the process—it's a lucky thing I live on the West Coast!*

To Jamie Saxon of the Philip Lief Group and Marlene Brown, *for their help and dedication in pulling the whole book together. Thanks for the hard work.*

To Arthur Gregory. *I saved him for last. A friend like Arthur comes once in a lifetime. I have received a lot of support throughout my life, but none like I have experienced with him. Thanks, Arthur. We both know I wouldn't be here if it weren't for you. I love you.*

Contents

Introduction

Cooking for family and friends has always made me happy. It's the one thing I know I'm really good at, and it brings me nothing but joy when I hear people raving about the food. Ever since I can remember they have asked me, "When are you going to write a cookbook?" I would always laugh and say, "I'm working on one." This book has been a lifetime in the making. I have included some recipes from my television show, Home & Family, because the response I get from viewers is truly overwhelming, and it's probably the biggest factor in my sitting down and finally putting this book together.

Food is a passion for me, integral to every aspect of my life, so I was not interested in just jotting down a few recipes. I thought if I showed a year's worth of meal-centered celebrations, explained the traditions, and shared some of the stories, it might make the food seem a little more real, the decorating a little less intimidating. I wanted to tell how and why we do certain things in our family. Why eating together is so important. The joy of setting a beautiful table. How our guests react to a crazy night with the Ferrare-Thomopouloses.

The sharing of experiences and the satisfaction of preparing delicious food and decorating to serve it can bring enormous enjoyment to your family life. Everyone who comes to our home knows they will have an authentic homemade meal, whether it's Italian, Chinese, Mexican, or whatever I'm in the mood for. I know our guests look forward to the meal with great anticipation, and it makes me feel so good. It's my way of showing how much I love my family and friends. It's something I feel I can give them from my heart.

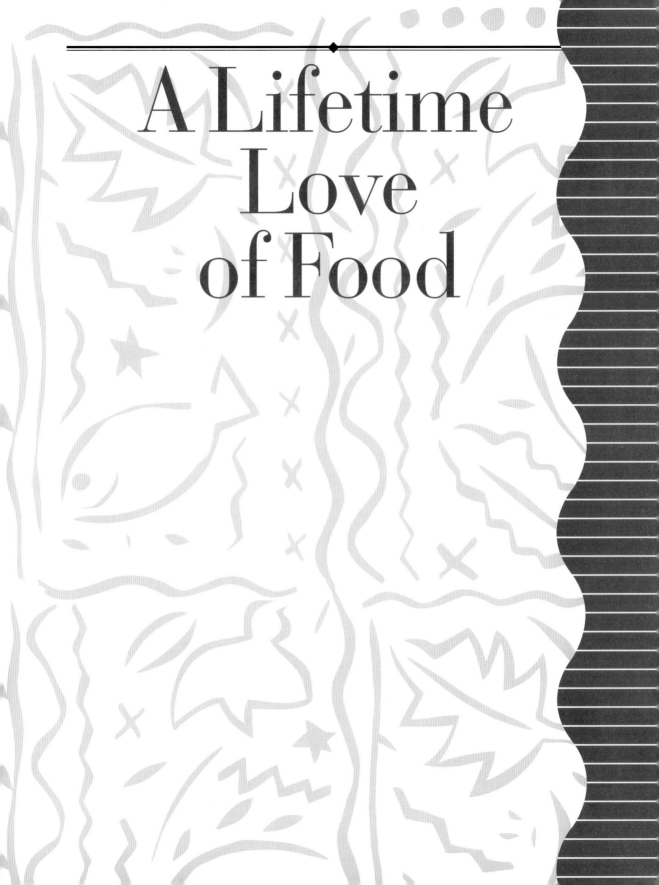

A Lifetime
Love
of Food

I love food! I love to look at it, smell it, cook it, and most of all, eat it! Nothing brings me more pleasure than to prepare a meal, whether it is a simple dinner or an all-out extravaganza. The whole ritual excites me, from planning the meal to setting the table.

This love affair with food goes way back to before I can remember, when my mother gave me my first taste of pastina, little star-shaped pasta that tasted *so* good. Mom used to prepare it in a hearty chicken soup, a delicate tomato sauce, or my favorite, butter and cheese. I call it a feel-good food because it always made me feel warm, loved, and satisfied. As a child I didn't mind getting sick, because the first thing I would get was a big bowl of pastina! Now, whenever my own kids are feeling down, the first thing they ask me is, "Can I have a bowl of pastina?"

In fact, it's the first real food I had after the bottle. We have a tradition in our family that the grandmother comes over to serve the first mouthful of these delightful morsels when the baby is only three weeks old. Too early, you say? Not for me! We have been doing this for generations, and all I know is that my kids slept through the night at three and a half weeks. I still eat pastina to this day, and it is undoubtedly my favorite.

My mother, Renata Ferrare, feeding Alexandra her first pastina.

So, my love affair with food started at one month. Eating was always a happy occasion in my family. When company was coming, which was all the time, you could feel the anticipation in the air. My younger sister, Diana, and my younger brother, Gino, would get so excited. (No one messed with me when I said I had a brother named Gino!) It meant good times, with singing, dancing, and great food. I loved helping in the kitchen any way I could, except doing the dishes. I did everything I could to get out of it. I volunteered to watch baby

Gino, or complained that my thyroid was hurting while I held my stomach. I would lock myself in the bathroom for what seemed like hours, and emerge to find the dishes waiting for me.

My parents, my younger sister, Diana, and I at a birthday party.

My mother and grandmother would sit down and plan the menu and where we would eat it. We had several choices in our house in suburban Cleveland. In the kitchen? Too small. In the dining room? Oh, no, no one eats there—someone might spill something! We ate in the basement. But this wasn't any dark, musty basement. My father spent what seemed like a year laying a beautiful floor with green and white tiles, and then he painted the cinder blocks lime green. Once he put in a stove and a refrigerator, we were cooking! We had a pool table in the basement, and this substituted as both a Ping-Pong table and a buffet table. This table would be filled with food for days on end.

Our neighbors thought we Ferrares were a little strange. We didn't build a garage, and we used the space to grow our own vegetables. I thought our garden was magical, because everything tasted so different from what my friends ate. We grew fresh basil and parsley, and my grandmother would chop these incredibly aromatic herbs by hand to make pesto. The whole house would smell like perfume from the earth. After she had minced the herbs really fine, she would chop up a whole head of garlic, put everything in a glass jar, and fill the jar with virgin olive oil. We would pour this over pasta cooked *al dente* and enjoy a heady summer meal. The word spread fast that the Ferrares were weird because we ate green spaghetti! But once the neighbors tasted the strange green substance, they loved it. Our whole family laughed about ten years ago when this "new" California cuisine hit really big, and all of a sudden pesto was the rage. Everyone was eating it!

My mother and grandmother prepared all the meals at my house, and I would watch intently as they sliced and diced, mixed and sautéed all these wonderful ingredients, and they would always come up with an outstanding dish. I worked at the kitchen sink, on salad detail. I hated it, because back then there was nothing inventive about salads the way there is today. I wanted to create. I wanted to cook on the stove and sauté the garlic in olive oil that always left such a delicious aroma. For some reason, I always thought I could do it better, so when Mom and Nony weren't looking I would go in and doctor up the recipe. I got nailed one time when Dad, who was looking forward to his pasta dinner, took one bite and promptly spit it out. What had gone wrong? As it turned out, after the sauce had already been cooked to perfection, I decided

Nony and Mom, September 1960.

that it really needed more tomato paste. I had secretly opened two cans of thick, raw paste and stirred them into the sauce. Have you ever tasted raw tomato paste? I was so disappointed when my dad didn't like it that I decided then and there to watch, listen, and learn before I tried things on my own.

I was about twelve years old when my mother did an incredibly wonderful thing for me. She actually allowed me to do the grocery shopping for her! On my way to the market with my list in hand, I stopped at the local five-and-dime, sat down at the counter, and ordered a grilled-cheese sandwich and a Coke. I wolfed it down because I wasn't supposed to be there, but I couldn't resist that gooey sandwich.

Once at the market, I was in heaven. I loved the experience of selecting fresh produce, and I was never too shy to ask questions, especially when it came to picking the right vegetables. I could never go wrong in the meat department,

*Cleveland, 1964. Is that
really me?*

because my dad was the meat cutter there, and would
always make sure I had the best. But my favorite thing to
do was to punch holes in the ground beef packages
when no one was looking!

When I was done leaving little holes in the meat,
I trotted off to finish the shopping. I went to the cashier and
paid with a check that my mother had signed. Forty-two dollars for only seven
bags of groceries? What was the world coming to? I quickly called a cab so that
I could get home and help my mom start cooking.

I've been very fortunate in my life, and have had opportunities to do what
I love to do. I started working very young. We moved to Los Angeles when
I was fourteen, and I came home from school one afternoon to find Mom having
coffee with a new friend. The friend told Mom I should be modeling, and that
she could introduce me to the right people. I met with Nina Blanchard, a very
important agent for modeling (and a life-long friend), the next week.

I remember it as if it were yesterday. I wore an empire-waist navy
blue jumpsuit with a white Peter Pan collar. My hair fell down my back in soft
curls. I looked like Wendy waiting for one of the Lost Boys to rescue me! Nina
told me to lose ten pounds, and signed me on the spot. I didn't lose the weight,
and worked on and off for several months doing local shoots. I got my break
when I was sixteen, and someone from Max Factor Cosmetics saw me. I did an
ad for them, and ended up under contract with them, working as the Max Factor
Girl. However, I didn't hit the big time until I moved to New York at age twenty,
after I finished school. Eileen Ford (another treasured friend) signed me,
and she said I had to lose ten pounds!

My really big break came when I went to see Francesco Scavullo, the hot,

My modeling years.

hot photographer who did all the covers of *Cosmopolitan* and the editorial pages for *Vogue.* When my picture hit the stands three months later, I was set for life. I never did lose that weight, and was successful in spite of it. In the age of Twiggy, I went against the modeling stereotype. Food and cooking were just too important to me.

My career as a model lasted almost twenty years. During that time I had two beautiful children, Zachary and Kathryn, and did some film work and guest spots on hit television shows. But through it all, I always took the time after work to stop at the market to bring home that evening's groceries and do what I love—cook! My reputation preceded me at modeling shoots, and I always brought some goodies with me. People who were invited to my house always knew they would eat well.

I have cooked for two people, and for as many as three hundred, thanks to my friend Eileen. She called me one day in 1983, depressed because she had just gotten off the phone with a caterer and was shocked at what he would charge for her daughter's wedding. The price quoted was $10,000. Yikes! Eileen really didn't know how to tell her daughter that she didn't want to pay that much. She tried other caterers, and they all came in at about that price range.

"Oh, for heaven's sake, Eileen," I said. "I'll cook for you, and it will cost you a whole lot less!" As a matter of fact, the whole thing came to less than a thousand dollars for three hundred people, not including wine. Impossible, you say? Not if pasta is the mainstay of your menu. I served four different kinds of pasta, sausage and peppers, several different salads, great breads, and ripe imported cheeses. The guests loved it, and thought that the fact that a real person had prepared it put a whole different spin on the evening. Everyone felt relaxed because they were eating homemade food.

My husband, Tony, and I have been married for thirteen happy years, blessed with mutual love and respect for one another. He is my best friend, truly my better half. I aspire to be like him but fall short in so many ways. I have never met anyone who even comes close to being the kind of person Tony is— loving, supportive, nonjudgmental, giving, self-sacrificing. I'm very proud of Tony and proud to be his wife. I have always thought of myself as independent and self-sufficient, but I notice that when Tony isn't around I feel a little empty and scared. I guess this comes from years of being so close to someone that you really become one in spirit.

The love we feel for our family motivates our very being. We have seven children and a grandchild! Tony has three kids from his first marriage—

Tony surrounded by excited kids at Christmas!

Anne, Denis, and Mark. I have my two from my first marriage—Zachary and Kathryn. And we share two together—Alexandra and Arianna. Anne is married to our handsome son-in-law, Patrice, and mother to our beautiful granddaughter, Claire. Our lives are filled with joy as we look at what we have been given. We thank God every single day for each other, our children, and the life we live. We take nothing for granted, especially each other.

*E*veryone always asks me how I find the time to do all the things I do! The question always surprises me, because I don't feel overwhelmed by my schedule, although it's quite full. I am a creature of habit—quite punctual and extremely organized. That is probably why I get so many things accomplished in one day. Do I get tired and cranky sometimes? Sure, every day—but boy, do I love what I do!

I host a two-hour talk show Monday through Friday, called *Home & Family.* I wake up at 5:00 A.M. three mornings a week to get in an hour of exercise, and I head in to work at 6:30. I love hosting my show, and I adore the people I work with. It makes it a joy to get up every day. My partner and cohost of *Home & Family,* Michael Burger, is a dream come true. I can always count on his support and his sense of humor. When I roll out of bed in the morning, I literally can't wait to see him, because I know he will bring out the best in me.

I arrive at the studio about 7:00 A.M., and meet with Arthur Gregory to go over the day's schedule. Arthur has been my manager for more than thirty years. He helps keep my life in order, and I don't take for granted one second how fortunate I am to have him in my life. After I know what to expect that day I go into makeup, which usually takes a whole hour. It's pure torture for me, because I've been made up thousands of times in my life. To break up the tedium, my makeup artist, Christina Sullivan, puts catalogs in front of my face. I circle the things I want, but don't order them. It keeps me quiet and sitting still!

Before I go into rehearsal I head back to my trailer to call the children and Tony and make sure that everything is all right at home. During the school year Tony and I have a pact. He stays home in the morning to send the kids off to school. Our kids are our first priority, always!

At 8:30 Michael and I go over each segment with our producers and block for cameras (choreograph the segments for the cameramen). At 9:30 I head back to the trailer to get dressed and touched up before we go on live at 10:00. There is always a sense of excitement and tension when I walk into the house and everyone is there. We know pretty much what will happen, but no matter how much we prepare it never turns out exactly the way we planned it, because our guests bring their own sense of style and way of doing things. It keeps the show spontaneous and fresh. Family members and guests are seated on the couch, along

Me with my cohost on Home & Family, Michael Burger.

with anyone else who happens to be around, with the crew and producers crowding around and Woody Fraser, our executive producer, telling me I should go change my outfit because I look terrible in the one I have on! After a quick prayer—"Please, God, bless this show and help us get through it!"—we're on!

Believe me, there isn't another show like *Home & Family!* Woody had the brilliant idea of building a real house instead of coming to you from a studio soundstage. Anything that happens in real life happens right on our show. Laughing, crying, heated discussions, disagreements, practical jokes, singing, games, and of course, cooking! Our show is part of the tram tour for Universal Studios, and the people get off and sit in for a segment of our show, so we get a new audience every day. The people in our television audience can call, fax, and e-mail us while we're on the air, and we constantly interact with them, getting ideas, praise, complaints—you name it!

We've shared much over the past year with our cast, staff, and crew—some of the best people in the business. We've brought children into the world with all the joy that it brings, and experienced heartache and tears when we've lost members of our team through death. We've shared everything with our audience, which is like our extended family. During the summer months, my kids sometimes even come to work with me, and we all love it! As a matter of fact, anyone on our staff or crew is welcome to bring his or her kids to the set. I particularly love it when during the broadcast one or several of the kids just barge right into the house wanting a glass of water. It all goes out live, just like at home! Being live is the only way to go. It keeps you alert and on the edge, and if you goof up or make a mistake (which I do, every day), it only makes it more like real life! The joy this job brings me is unlike anything I have ever experienced in my long career. To touch people and communicate with one another is so rewarding.

Everyone looks forward to our cooking segments, especially our cast and crew, who wait anxiously for the segment to be over so they can devour all the food. It is always beautifully and professionally prepared by our executive chef, Jamie Gwen, who takes my recipes and presents them in such a way that it's

almost a shame to eat them.
We skipped the cooking
segment twice because we
thought we had too much
material for the show, and you
would not believe the mail
and calls we got from viewers!
Cooking is definitely every-

Michael "helping" me cook on Home & Family.

one's favorite segment, so now we make sure to do it every day.

Because our show is interactive, our audience can e-mail us with great
kitchen tips and ideas. Two of my favorites: use an egg slicer to cut kiwi,
strawberries, and bananas, and use uncooked linguine to hold food together
if you're out of toothpicks.

Two hours pass quickly. Before I know it it is noon, and we are off the air.
I make a quick call to Tony to find out if he saw this morning's show and ask
him what he thought. Mike and I tape our promos—mini-commercials for the
next day's show—and by 12:30 we are finished. I have an hour to catch my
breath and have some lunch, then head to a meeting at 1:30 to go over the next
day's show. I leave the studio at 2:30 and do my errands, or simply head home
to paint my pottery, which I love to do more than almost anything—except being
a wife and mother, doing *Home & Family*, grocery shopping, cooking, and
eating! I love being and doing all these things with such a passion, and you can
always find the time to do the things that make you happy.

When the kids come home from school around 4:30, I prepare them
a quick snack, and they do their homework until dinner. Arianna, my youngest
daughter, loves to cook, and Alexandra is showing a lot more interest, which
thrills me, because I love having them in the kitchen helping me.

After dinner we have family time. We read, play board games, or have what I call "stupid night," just chilling and watching TV. At 9:00 it's lights out, and Tony and I have a chance to catch up on what has been happening in our lives. With all that is going on, we have a lot to talk about!

The weekends are always devoted to our kids, with soccer, tennis, swimming, and food shopping. We never know who will show up for dinner. Our kids have a lot of friends, and they are always welcome. We have a full house all the time, but once in a while Tony and I do manage to go out and have grown-up time. What a concept! Sometimes it is hard to keep my eyes open, but when I sleep, it's always sweet. The many hours I put into my day are totally worth it, and I can't imagine doing anything else.

Cooking for a crowd is always an adventure!

A Year Full of Holidays

New Year's Eve

Osso Buco

Risotto

Pastina con Brodo with Chicken Meatballs

Chocolate Mousse Cake

Osso Buco (page 18),
Risotto (page 19).

*N*ew Year's Eve is always exciting. My parents insisted that wherever they went for New Year's Eve, my sister, brother, and I had to go as well. We would go in our jammies to the house where the party was and spend the evening in a bedroom, playing and watching TV with the other kids. All we could think about was the food. We couldn't wait till Mom brought us some from the buffet. Then we would celebrate— Mom, Dad, Diana, Gino, and me. A kiss goodnight, and we were dozing! All I could think about before falling asleep was what I would someday serve at my own New Year's Eve dinner. I've come a long way from wanting to serve Oscar Meyer wieners, french fries, and onion rings with all-you-can-drink Coca-Cola!

Now that my younger kids can stay up past twelve o'clock, they bring in the New Year with Tony and me. We usually spend the holiday in Sun Valley, Idaho, with some of our closest friends. Sun Valley is a small town that looks as if it is right out of a painting, quaint and traditional, and the people are warm and friendly. There is always a lot of snow on the ground, the air is crisp and cold, and the atmosphere is still festive from Christmas, with lights everywhere.

I always consider it a great compliment when my friends want me to cook for them, so we often celebrate New Year's with dinner either at our house or at a friend's house. If we go to a friend's house, I will contribute to the evening by bringing a dish or two, or sometimes even the whole meal! The children are so excited about staying up late that they actually stay out of our hair and find ways to entertain themselves until dinner, while the guys gather to play pool and to conspire to keep the women from playing—they know we'll beat them, and they can't stand it! The whole evening is filled with a special feeling, and we give thanks for our children, good friends, and good times.

We start the dinner at about ten o'clock, and sit at tables that have been set with our best china and crystal. The kids finish first and run to play and watch videos, and we adults eat, laugh, and talk, talk, talk until midnight, when we turn on the TV to watch Dick Clark's Rockin' New Year's Eve. *Then, as we watch the ball drop in Times Square from the comfort of our living room, I kiss my husband with our two youngest girls standing between us. (We call this our "family sandwich.") I am always filled with emotion as I wish for nothing but good things for my family and friends in the coming year. Of course, the one thing I wish most of all is for all of our children to be in one place at the same time. What a perfect evening that would be!*

Osso Buco

¼ *cup olive oil*

6 garlic cloves, smashed

6 veal shanks, cut 1½ inches
   thick

All-purpose flour for coating

½ *cup sherry*

Juice of 2 lemons

3 to 4 cups chicken stock

Salt and freshly ground pepper
   to taste

½ *cup fresh Italian parsley,*
   chopped for garnish

1 tablespoon lemon zest
   for garnish

In a deep sauté pan, heat the oil, add the garlic, and sauté until lightly golden. Remove the garlic.

Dredge each shank in flour and shake off the excess. Add the shanks to the pan and brown on all sides. Add the sherry, and reduce slightly for about 1 minute. Add the lemon juice and stock. Cook over low to medium heat until the meat is tender and falls off the bone, about 1½ hours. Remove the shanks, skim the fat from the pan, and season with salt and pepper. Over medium heat, allow the liquid to thicken enough to coat a spoon. If you have trouble thickening the sauce, try dissolving 1 tablespoon arrowroot in ¼ cup water and whisk it into the sauce. Return the shanks to the pan and coat with the sauce. Garnish with the chopped parsley and lemon zest. Serve with risotto (recipe follows).

6 servings

Risotto

3 cups chicken stock or water

2 cups water

½ teaspoon saffron or turmeric

2 tablespoons olive oil

2 tablespoons unsalted butter

1 medium onion, chopped

1½ cups Arborio rice

1 cup white wine

½ cup grated Parmesan cheese

½ teaspoon salt

¼ teaspoon freshly ground
   pepper

Combine broth, water, and saffron in a saucepan and bring to a boil. Cover and keep warm over medium heat.

In a large skillet, heat the oil and butter. Add the onion and sauté until tender. Add the rice and stir to coat. Stir in the wine and bring the mixture to a boil; reduce heat. Add just enough of the broth mixture to cover the rice. Cook over low heat, stirring constantly, until the liquid evaporates. Add more broth mixture just to cover rice. Continue cooking, stirring constantly, until all of the liquid is incorporated and cooked away and the rice is tender, about 15 to 20 minutes. Stir in the Parmesan, salt, and pepper and serve.

8 side-dish servings

Pastina con Brodo with Chicken Meatballs

It will warm your insides.

Cristina's chicken stock

One 3- to 3½-pound chicken

2 onions, halved

3 celery stalks

6 carrots, peeled

8 sprigs of parsley

Water to cover

Soup

2 scallions, chopped

6 sprigs of parsley, chopped

1 tablespoon Italian parsley
   (optional)

1 large egg

1 tablespoon soy sauce

½ cup grated Romano cheese

1 teaspoon salt

¼ teaspoon freshly ground
   pepper

Reserved chicken stock

1½ cups pastina, little stars,
   or orzo

Fresh chopped chives or parsley
   for garnish

For the chicken stock. In an 8-quart stockpot, place the chicken, onions, celery, carrots, and parsley. Add about 5 quarts water, enough to cover the chicken by at least 2 inches. Bring mixture to a boil; reduce heat. Simmer, partially covered, until chicken is tender, about 1 hour. Strain chicken and vegetables, reserving stock. Measure 4 quarts of chicken stock (add canned chicken broth if necessary to make 4 quarts) and return to the stockpot. Discard vegetables. Remove meat from the chicken and reserve. Discard skin and bones.

For the soup. Tear the meat into bite-size pieces and place in a food processor with the scallions, parsley, egg, soy sauce, Romano cheese, salt, and pepper. Process until well blended. Shape mixture into 1-inch meatballs, about the size of a purple grape. Set aside.

Cook the pastina or desired pasta according to the package directions and drain. Meanwhile, bring the reserved chicken stock to a boil. Reduce heat to simmer and add the meatballs. Simmer for 10 minutes, but do not boil, since this will break up the meatballs. Rinse the cooked pastina and add to the soup, then season with salt and pepper to taste. Garnish with chopped fresh chives and chopped fresh parsley.

10 to 12 servings

Chocolate Mousse Cake

This cake is extremely rich and tastes like a chocolate truffle.

Cake

Two 8-ounce packages semisweet chocolate

2 cups (4 sticks) unsalted butter

1 cup sugar

1 cup half-and-half or light cream

1 tablespoon vanilla extract

¼ teaspoon salt

8 large eggs, lightly beaten

Glaze

One 6-ounce package semisweet chocolate pieces

½ cup (1 stick) unsalted butter

1 tablespoon milk

2 tablespoons light corn syrup

Whipped cream garnish

1 cup heavy cream

1 tablespoon sugar

1 teaspoon vanilla extract

Preheat the oven to 350°F.

In a double boiler or a small heavy saucepan, heat together the semisweet chocolate, butter, sugar, half-and-half, vanilla, and salt over medium-low heat. Stir until the chocolate melts and the mixture is smooth.

In a separate bowl, beat the eggs until light. Stir in about ½ cup of the melted chocolate mixture, whisking quickly, then gradually stir the remaining warm chocolate mixture into the eggs until blended. Pour into a greased 10 x 3-inch springform pan.

Bake 50 to 60 minutes, or until a toothpick inserted into the center of the cake comes out clean. (The cake gets puffy at the edges, then sinks during cooling.) Cool completely. Remove pan sides, cover in plastic wrap, and refrigerate for 6 hours.

For the glaze. In a double boiler or a small heavy saucepan over low heat, melt the semisweet chocolate pieces and butter, stirring frequently until melted and smooth. Remove from the heat. Stir in the corn syrup and milk until well blended.

Cristina Ferrare's Family Entertaining

Unwrap the cake and place it on a serving platter. Spread with the warm glaze. If not serving immediately, refrigerate the cake until ready to serve.

For whipped cream garnish. Beat the heavy cream on high speed with an electric mixer until stiff peaks form, then fold in the sugar and vanilla. Pipe a design over the top of the cake, or spoon cream over each serving.

16 servings

Super Bowl Party

Marinated Beef

Red-and-White Slaw

Sausage and Peppers

Antipasto Sandwiches

Kick-butt Chili

Spicy Piquant Chicken

Turkey Pinwheel Sandwiches

Double Trouble Chocolate Bars

Kick-butt Chili (page 30).

I love football! Everyone gathers at our house for yelling, screaming, jumping, and eating! I don't think I have ever watched the halftime activities because everyone makes a beeline for the kitchen. I usually try to cut the edge of hunger for our guests by serving homemade soft pretzels during the first half.

I like to have a bit of variety in my Super Bowl menu because football isn't just for men anymore. I for one love the game, and so do my girlfriends. God forbid you should ask me for anything while the game is going on. However, when halftime comes I'm ready to roll. I have everything prepared ahead of time so that I can go straight to the fridge and the oven and place everything on the buffet table. I keep everything on the table through the fourth quarter for those who like to perpetually nosh, and for any stragglers who show up because they know there's plenty of food at the Ferrare-Thomopouloses.

Marinated Beef

½ cup soy sauce

½ cup Worcestershire sauce

½ cup balsamic vinegar

2 tablespoons celery seed

1 tablespoon garlic salt

1 tablespoon onion salt

2 tablespoons freshly ground pepper

1½ pounds sirloin steak

Arugula or mixed greens

Preheat the broiler. Combine all the ingredients except the steak and arugula and marinate steak for at least 1 hour. Grill to desired doneness. Slice thin and serve on a bed of arugula or mixed greens.

4 servings

Red-and-White Slaw

½ small head red cabbage, shredded

½ medium head white cabbage, shredded

¼ cup sour cream

¼ cup Miracle Whip or mayonnaise

Juice of ½ lemon

3 tablespoons poppy seeds

Place the cabbage in a large bowl. Add the sour cream, Miracle Whip or mayonnaise, lemon juice, and poppy seeds. Combine well, coating the cabbage. Refrigerate for 30 minutes before serving.

16 servings

Sausage and Peppers

6 green bell peppers

2 red bell peppers

8 hot or mild Italian sausages

¼ cup olive oil

6 garlic cloves, thinly sliced

½ teaspoon hot red pepper flakes

One cup of your favorite tomato
sauce

¼ cup water

1 teaspoon salt

¼ teaspoon freshly ground
pepper

12 French bread slices, toasted

Chopped parsley for garnish

Preheat the broiler. Place the bell peppers on a broiler pan and roast about 4 inches from the heat, turning frequently with tongs, until charred on all sides. Remove the peppers and place them in a brown paper bag. Close the bag and allow the peppers to steam for 10 to 15 minutes. Pull off and discard the skin from the peppers; remove stems and seeds. Cut each pepper into six slices and set aside.

Place sausages in a large, deep skillet. Fill the skillet with water until the sausages are almost covered and bring to a boil for 20 minutes or until the water evaporates. Brown the sausages on all sides. Remove from heat. Cut each sausage with 3 diagonal cuts to make 4 pieces. Set aside.

In the same skillet, heat the remaining 2 tablespoons of oil. Sauté the garlic until tender, then stir in the sliced peppers and red pepper flakes. Cook, stirring frequently, until the peppers are tender, about 7 to 10 minutes. Combine the tomato sauce and ¼ cup water and stir into the pepper mixture along with the salt and pepper. Add the sausages. Simmer, covered, 10 minutes more, or until the sausages are done. For each serving, spoon mixture over two slices of toasted French bread. Garnish with chopped parsley.

6 servings

Cristina Ferrare's Family Entertaining

Antipasto Sandwiches

You can buy roasted red peppers in Italian markets or the gourmet section of larger supermarkets, or use the procedure on p. 143.

2 large (1 to 1½ pounds each) round sourdough loaves

¼ cup Dijon mustard

8 ounces sliced Genoa or cotto salami

8 ounces sliced Monterey Jack cheese

¼ cup olive oil

2 cups roasted red peppers, drained

½ cup crumbled goat cheese

½ cup mayonnaise

½ pound sliced prosciutto or ham

½ pound sliced mortadella or muenster cheese

2 cups arugula or torn spinach leaves

Additional mayonnaise, if desired

Preheat the oven to 350°F. To crisp the bread, place the loaves directly on the oven rack for 10 minutes. Slice each loaf horizontally into four slices.

To assemble the sandwiches, place both bottom slices side by side on a flat surface. Spread each with Dijon mustard. Top with the salami and Monterey Jack cheese slices. Place the next bread layer on top of each bottom layer. Brush with the olive oil. Top with the roasted peppers and goat cheese. Top with the third bread layer. Spread with mayonnaise. Layer on the prosciutto and mortadella slices, then the arugula or spinach. If desired, spread mayonnaise on the inside of the bread tops. Place the tops cut side down over each sandwich stack. Wrap the whole sandwiches tightly in plastic wrap. Refrigerate for 1 hour to allow the flavors to blend. To serve, cut each sandwich into 8 pie-shaped wedges; secure each wedge with a frilly party pick if desired.

16 servings

Kick-butt Chili

2 tablespoons olive oil

2 pounds sirloin steak,
cut into ½-inch cubes

2 medium onions, chopped

3 garlic cloves, minced

1 jalapeño pepper, seeded
and minced

2 tablespoons chili powder

1 tablespoon cumin

1½ teaspoons cayenne pepper

Two 28-ounce cans diced
tomatoes, undrained

1 cup canned red kidney beans,
drained and rinsed

Salt and freshly ground pepper
to taste

Sour cream, chopped onions,
shredded cheddar cheese, or
sliced scallions for garnish

Heat the oil in a large heavy pot. Brown the steak cubes on all sides and remove from the pan. In the pan drippings sauté the onions, garlic, and jalapeño until the onions are tender. Stir in the chili powder, cumin, cayenne, tomatoes, beans, and browned meat. Simmer the mixture, uncovered, over low heat for 1 hour. Uncover and simmer until the chili is the desired consistency, about 30 minutes more. Season with salt and pepper. Serve the chili with desired garnishes.

6 to 7 servings

Spicy Piquant Chicken

½ cup olive oil

Two 3- to 3½-pound frying
   chickens, cut up

2 onions, chopped

2 cups chopped celery

1 red bell pepper, cut into
   ½-inch pieces

1 green bell pepper, cut into
   ½-inch pieces

¼ cup all-purpose flour

Two 28-ounce cans crushed
   tomatoes

1 cup chicken broth

One 6-ounce can tomato paste

3 tablespoons lemon juice

1 teaspoon hot red pepper flakes

1 teaspoon freshly ground pepper

½ to 1 teaspoon hot pepper
   sauce

4 garlic cloves, minced

1 bay leaf

4 scallions, chopped

16 spicy green or green pimiento-
   stuffed olives, sliced

2 tablespoons chopped parsley

Sour cream (optional)

Hot cooked rice

In a stockpot, heat the oil. Brown the chicken pieces on all sides. Remove from the pan and set aside. In the same pan, sauté the onions, celery, and bell peppers until tender. Remove them and set aside. Drain off all but 1 tablespoon of fat from the pan. Stir in the flour, scraping the crusty bits from the bottom of the pan. Stir in the crushed tomatoes, chicken broth, tomato paste, lemon juice, red pepper flakes, pepper, hot pepper sauce, garlic, bay leaf, and cooked vegetables. Bring the mixture to a boil, then reduce the heat. Add the chicken pieces and simmer, partially covered, until sauce is thick, about 1 hour. Remove the bay leaf and skim off excess fat. Stir in the scallions, sliced olives, and parsley just before serving. Garnish each serving with a dollop of sour cream, if desired. Serve with hot cooked rice.

8 to 9 servings

Turkey Pinwheel Sandwiches

Lavosh bread is an Armenian flat bread, found in specialty markets. Flour tortillas are a great substitute.

2 pieces lavosh bread, or six 8-inch flour tortillas

12 ounces low-fat cream cheese, softened

2 tablespoons minced fresh herbs, such as basil, dill, oregano, chives, sage, or marjoram

1½ cups torn fresh spinach or arugula leaves

8 ounces sliced turkey breast

Roll up the lavosh or stack the tortillas and wrap in foil. Warm in a 300°F oven for 15 minutes.

Stir together the cream cheese and herbs. Remove the bread from the oven and gently spread one side of each piece of lavosh or each tortilla with some of the cream cheese mixture. Cover with a layer of spinach or arugula, and top with turkey slices. Roll up each bread piece or tortilla and slice crosswise into 1-inch slices. Serve immediately.

16 pinwheel sandwiches with lavosh bread or
32 smaller sandwiches with tortillas

Double Trouble Chocolate Bars

½ cup (1 stick) unsalted butter, softened

1 cup firmly packed dark brown sugar

1 large egg

1 teaspoon vanilla extract

1½ cups all-purpose flour

1 cup quick-cooking rolled oats

½ teaspoon baking soda

One 6-ounce package (1 cup) semisweet chocolate morsels

¾ cup peanut butter chips

½ cup peanut halves

Preheat the oven to 350°F.

In a large mixing bowl, beat together the softened butter, brown sugar, egg, and vanilla on medium speed of electric mixer until well blended. Stir in flour, oats, and baking soda until well combined (mixture will be stiff). Reserve one-third of the oatmeal mixture. Press remaining mixture in the bottom of a 12 x 8-inch baking dish. Sprinkle chocolate morsels, peanut butter chips, and peanuts evenly over cookie layer. Crumble remaining oatmeal mixture evenly over chocolate-peanut layer. Bake for 25 to 30 minutes or until top is light golden brown. Allow bars to cool completely; cut into squares.

12 to 16 bars

Valentine's Day

Chicken Piccata over Mashed Potatoes

Asparagus Tips with Cucumber Vinaigrette

Endive Lettuce with
Walnut-Gorgonzola Dressing

Tiramisù with Homemade Mascarpone

Tiramisù with Homemade Mascarpone (page 42).
Heart-shaped plates by Cristina.

My kids love Valentine's Day. They get so excited making cards for their dad, grandparents, and special friends. They give store-bought cards to their school friends, with heart-shaped message candies that say "I LUV U" or "KISS ME" included in the envelopes. We also make cupcakes and decorate them with the name of each child in their class.

We make photo keepsakes for grandparents and other special people. Glue a heart-shaped doily on top of a piece of colored construction paper that is cut to the size of whatever frame you are using. Then center a favorite photograph over the doily and glue it in place. Dry thoroughly, then insert into the frame. Another way to present these photos is to glue dried flowers around the border of the glass of the frame. Insert the photograph in the center. The effect is beautiful and different. Dried rose or pansy petals work the best. You can buy them at a craft supply store, or dry them yourself with a product called silica gel.

Valentine's Day dinner is always elegant and pretty. I set the table with lace. You can go to the fabric store and buy remnants of three or four yards of lace and use it for a tablecloth. If you have a pretty solid-color tablecloth, say in pink or green, you can lay the lace over it for a lovely effect. Set the table with candles, of course—heart-shaped if they're available.

For the flowers, I recycle an old favorite of mine. Take four to six small juice glasses, and line each with a piece of old lace or cotton handkerchief so that the fabric edges fall prettily over the glass edge. Arrange dried flowers in each glass, and tie pink or white ribbon gently around the glasses. I use these arrangements on my table all year long, and just change the ribbon according to the occasion.

I use heart-shaped dinner, salad, and dessert plates that I painted myself. Each plate is painted differently, but when they are on the table together they blend beautifully. I get a great deal of satisfaction when I look at the table after it has been set with my own creations.

Don't be intimidated—it's really very easy to make your own plates. First, locate a store that does ceramics. Most cities now have places where pottery is made; I use the Klay Kitchen in Los Angeles. Ask the clerk at the ceramics store if they have heart-shaped plates, or if they could obtain a mold and pour them for you. Trace the plates on white paper, and draw an original design on the paper with a pencil until you're sure you know what you want. Then draw the same design on the plate with a pencil and paint the design on the plate using paints the store recommends. You can glaze it yourself or have the store do it. Be creative! And let the kids paint their own—they'll get a big kick out of eating off something they made.

Chicken Piccata over Mashed Potatoes

4 chicken breast halves, skinned,
   boned, and pounded to
   ¼-inch thickness
All-purpose flour for dredging
2 tablespoons olive oil
8 garlic cloves, smashed
1 lemon
½ cup dry sherry
¼ cup capers
Salt and freshly ground pepper to
   taste
Chopped parsley and lemon slices
   for garnish

Mashed potatoes
4 medium potatoes
2 tablespoons butter
⅓ cup warm low-fat milk
¼ teaspoon salt

Dredge the chicken in flour until coated, shaking off the excess.
Heat the oil in a sauté pan over medium-high heat, add the chicken and
garlic, and cook 2 minutes on each side. Squeeze the juice of 1 lemon over
the chicken. Add the sherry while scraping the bottom of the pan. Add
capers. Cook 3 minutes more and season with salt and pepper.

For the mashed potatoes. Wash the potatoes well and cut in half.
Place the potatoes in a saucepan and add enough water to cover. Bring
to a gentle boil and cook the potatoes until tender, about 20 to 25 minutes.
To test doneness, insert a knife into a potato; if it goes through without
any pressure, it is ready. Rinse the potatoes under cold running water and
peel. The skins should come off easily. Return the potatoes to the pot and
mash well with a potato masher to remove all the lumps or put through a

ricer. Turn the heat on low, add the butter, slowly pour in the milk, and then add the salt. Mix well.

For each serving, place one chicken breast half on a mound of mashed potatoes. Pour the sherry mixture over all, garnish with sliced lemon, and sprinkle parsley on top.

4 servings

Asparagus Tips with Cucumber Vinaigrette

3 bunches (3 to 3½ pounds)
asparagus
1 cup peeled, seeded, and
chopped cucumber
½ cup chopped red bell pepper
2 scallions, chopped
2 tablespoons chopped basil
2 tablespoons chopped Italian
parsley

½ cup olive oil
⅓ cup lemon juice
1 tablespoon Dijon mustard
1 teaspoon low-sodium soy sauce
Salt and freshly ground pepper
to taste

Snap off the tough ends of the asparagus. Steam the asparagus until crisp-tender, about 2-3 minutes. Place the spears on a serving platter.

In a medium bowl, stir together the cucumber, red pepper, scallions, basil, and parsley. In another small bowl, whisk together the oil, lemon juice, mustard, soy sauce, and salt and pepper to taste. Pour the dressing over the cucumber mixture and spoon this mixture over the asparagus. Sprinkle with parsley. Serve hot or at room temperature.

6 servings

Endive Lettuce with Walnut-Gorgonzola Dressing

6 heads endive lettuce, cut into
  julienne strips
½ cup walnut oil
¼ cup white wine vinegar
Juice of 1 lemon
1 tablespoon Dijon mustard

1 cup crumbled Gorgonzola
  cheese
1 cup Granny Smith apple, cubed
½ cup chopped walnuts
½ cup chopped Italian parsley

Wash the lettuce thoroughly and pat dry. Place the lettuce in a salad bowl and keep chilled until you are ready to serve.

Whisk together the oil, vinegar, lemon juice, and mustard. Pour over the lettuce and mix gently. Place on chilled plates and sprinkle with the cheese, apples, walnuts, and parsley. Toast some great bread and enjoy!

8 servings

Tiramisù with Homemade Mascarpone

Homemade mascarpone
Three 8-ounce packages light
cream cheese, softened
½ cup heavy cream
⅓ cup sour cream
Tiramisù
1½ cups powdered sugar
¼ cup Marsala wine
¾ cup heavy cream

⅔ cup water
5 teaspoons instant espresso
powder
Three 3-ounce packages
ladyfingers
Cocoa powder, fresh whole
strawberries, and/or mint
leaves for garnish

For the homemade mascarpone. Place the cream cheese, heavy cream, and sour cream in a food processor and process until smooth. (Or you can beat the ingredients together with an electric mixer until well blended.)

For the tiramisù. In a food processor, process the mascarpone with 1 cup of the powdered sugar and the wine until blended. Add the cream and process until blended. (Or you can use an electric mixer to combine ingredients.) Set aside.

In a small saucepan over high heat, combine the water, remaining ½ cup powdered sugar, and espresso powder. Bring to a boil, then remove from the heat. Cool 5 minutes.

In the bottom of a 13 x 9 x 2-inch baking dish or decorated shallow casserole dish, arrange a single layer of ladyfingers. Brush with some of the espresso syrup. Spread a third of the mascarpone mixture over. Repeat layers twice, ending with the mascarpone. Cover and refrigerate until firm. To serve, sift cocoa lightly over the top and spoon into serving dishes.

Garnish each serving with a whole strawberry and mint leaves, if desired. Will keep in the refrigerator for up to 2 days.

For individual tiramisùs. For eight or nine individual servings, use two 3-ounce packages ladyfingers. Prepare mascarpone mixture and espresso syrup as directed. Arrange eight or nine long-stemmed dessert goblets on a tray for ease in handling. Place 3 ladyfingers in the bottom of each goblet. Brush with the espresso syrup. Fill half of each goblet with mascarpone and top with a second layer of ladyfingers. Brush the ladyfingers with syrup, then spoon the remaining cheese mixture over. Cover the goblets and place the tray in the refrigerator until the tiramisù is firm. Garnish as directed above.

8 servings

Easter

Marinated Leg of Lamb

Orzo Salad

Sautéed Spinach

Roasted Baby New Potatoes

Italian Peas

Egg Salad Bunny

Rice Pudding

Banana Bread

Strawberry Charlotte

Marinated Leg of Lamb (page 48),
Orzo Salad (page 49),
Egg Salad Bunny (page 51).

*E*aster is an especially festive time in the Ferrare-Thomopoulos household. I start planning three or four weeks early! The first thing is the guest list. I have a very large family, and we have had up to fifty people at Easter dinner, so I need to figure out the food quantities and how many Easter baskets we'll need for the kids. I always add six or eight people in my planning, to account for last-minute additions.

As soon as the guest list is completed, I start to make Easter baskets for all the kids. I head down to the local craft store to purchase baskets, colored grass, yellow ribbon, and several dozen plastic eggs. I fill the eggs with little chocolates, pennies, and nickels—kids love money!—and place them in the grass-filled baskets. I top each basket off with a yellow ribbon. As the children arrive for dinner, I give each one a basket. When all the families arrive, we start our Easter egg hunt. We give the younger children a head start in finding eggs, and when we yell "go!" and signal the older kids, it's general mayhem, with kids screaming "I got one!" at the top of their lungs. I'm always amazed at how cleverly they manage to stuff eggs into their clothes after their Easter baskets are full. Once all the eggs are found, the kids run to their parents, quickly deposit their finds, and run off to play, never looking back. When it's time for dinner, they reemerge, and the proud parents have but a vague memory of how nice the kids looked when they first arrived in their Sunday finest!

With so many guests, I usually serve a buffet, and since we live in California, we have an advantage—we can eat outdoors. The main conversation piece of the buffet table is my

Arianna hunting for Easter eggs.

Cristina Ferrare's Family Entertaining

egg salad bunny, which I thought of as a way to use up Easter eggs. It's fun to watch the kids compete for the choicest bunny parts! We arrange tables of ten in our yard, and I use yellow or floral tablecloths. For each table I make a centerpiece by filling a large basket with colorful flowers, arranged to welcome springtime. For place settings, I mix and match, borrowing dishes from friends and relatives.

But if the weather is bad, we have to move everything inside. One year there was a downpour on Easter morning, and we had to accommodate fifty people in our house. Do you think everyone congregated in the living room, den, or dining room? No, of course not. They all wanted to be in the kitchen!

Marinated Leg of Lamb

8-pound leg of lamb (have the
    butcher take out the gland to
    avoid the gamey taste)
6 garlic cloves
1 teaspoon dried rosemary
Salt and freshly ground pepper
    to taste
½ cup Dijon mustard

Juice of 2 lemons
2 tablespoons olive oil
½ cup soy sauce
½ cup red wine or soy sauce
1 cup chicken stock or water
Fresh rosemary and chopped
    parsley for garnish

Puncture a finger-size hole in meat and place the garlic cloves inside. Sprinkle the rosemary, salt, and pepper over lamb. Mix together the mustard, lemon juice, olive oil, and soy sauce and marinate the lamb in the mixture in the refrigerator overnight.

One hour before cooking remove the lamb from the refrigerator. Preheat the oven to 350°F. Cook lamb covered with foil for 1 hour, then remove the foil. Insert a meat thermometer into the meat. Baste every 15 minutes until the lamb reaches an internal temperature of 145 to 150°F. This will take about 1½ hours. When the lamb is golden and crispy, pour the red wine or soy sauce over the meat. Remove from the oven, transfer to a platter, and let stand for 20 minutes before carving.

Add chicken stock or water to the juice in the baking pan. Heat over low heat, scraping to remove any bits from the pan. Strain and pour over the sliced lamb. Garnish with rosemary and chopped parsley.

8 servings

Cristina Ferrare's Family Entertaining

Orzo Salad

1 pound orzo

2 cucumbers, peeled, seeded,
   and diced

½ cup chopped fresh basil

4 celery stalks, diced

1 red pepper, seeded and
   chopped

1 cup cherry tomatoes, halved

2 tablespoons chopped fresh dill

2 tablespoons Dijon mustard

½ cup olive oil

Juice of 2 lemons

Salt and freshly ground pepper
   to taste

Cook the orzo in boiling salted water. Drain, rinse, and set aside.

In a salad bowl, combine the next 6 ingredients. Add the orzo and mix again. Combine the mustard and olive oil, whisking until blended. Add the lemon juice, salt, and pepper and mix well. Pour over the salad and mix well.

8 servings

Sautéed Spinach

1 pound spinach leaves, washed,
   stems removed

¼ cup olive oil

2 garlic cloves, minced

Juice of 1 lemon

Hot red pepper flakes to taste

Salt and freshly ground pepper
   to taste

Steam the spinach in the water that clings to the leaves for 30 seconds. Remove, drain, and squeeze dry. Heat the oil in a large sauté pan over medium heat. Sauté the garlic lightly, then add the spinach, lemon juice, and red pepper flakes. Season with salt and pepper.

4 servings

Roasted Baby New Potatoes

**30 new potatoes, halved and
    left unpeeled**
2 medium onions, thinly sliced
¼ cup olive oil

**Salt and freshly ground pepper
    to taste**
**1 tablespoon fresh rosemary
    leaves**

Preheat the oven to 325°F. Place the potatoes in a baking pan and cover with the onions. Drizzle oil over all. Add salt, pepper, and rosemary. Bake uncovered until crisp and golden, about 1 hour. Toss with a spatula several times for even cooking.

8 servings

Italian Peas

**Two 10-ounce packages frozen
    baby peas**
1 large yellow onion, thinly sliced
1 tomato, chopped
6 slices prosciutto, chopped

¼ cup water
1 tablespoon unsalted butter
Salt to taste
**½ teaspoon freshly ground
    pepper**

Mix all the ingredients except for the butter, salt, and pepper and cook over medium heat for 35 minutes. Before serving, stir in the butter, salt, and freshly ground pepper.

8 servings

Egg Salad Bunny

12 large eggs, hard-boiled
   and chopped
1 to 1¼ cups mayonnaise
½ red bell pepper, finely chopped
1 medium dill pickle, chopped
1 scallion, finely chopped
1 teaspoon yellow mustard
1 teaspoon lemon juice
¼ teaspoon salt
¼ teaspoon freshly ground
   pepper

¼ teaspoon curry powder
   (optional)
Lettuce leaves
Bunny decorations: romaine
   lettuce or Belgian endive,
   pimiento-stuffed green olive,
   ripe pitted olive, carrot, red
   bell pepper, finely chopped
   parsley, sprig of parsley, red
   radish, or your own
   decorations

In a large bowl, combine the chopped eggs with ½ cup of the mayonnaise, the red pepper, dill pickle, scallion, mustard, lemon juice, salt, pepper, and curry powder, if desired, until well combined.

To assemble the bunny, line a 16- to 18-inch platter or plastic wrap-covered baking sheet with lettuce leaves. Using your hands or a couple of large spoons, shape the egg salad into a bunny shape, forming the head, an oval-shaped body, ears, and small circles for the feet and paws. Then coat the bunny with the remaining mayonnaise, covering completely.

To decorate the bunny, use tiny lettuce leaves to accent the ears, and cut the green olive in half for the eyes. Use half a pitted ripe olive for the nose, slivers of carrot for the whiskers, a bell pepper strip for the necklace, and a small sprig of parsley for the necktie. Then cut two thin julienne strips of carrot for the suspenders, and coat the bottom half of the bunny's body with parsley for his pants. Place a radish slice under each foot. Cover loosely and refrigerate until serving time, up to 24 hours ahead.

4 to 6 servings

Rice Pudding

7 cups milk

2 cups heavy cream

1⅓ cups long grain rice

1 cup sugar

¾ cup raisins

¼ cup (½ stick) unsalted butter

3 large eggs

Ground cinnamon and whipped cream for garnish (optional)

In a 4-quart heavy pot combine the milk and heavy cream. Bring the mixture just to a boil over medium-high heat (small bubbles will appear around edge of pan), stirring frequently. Stir in the rice, sugar, raisins, and butter. Bring the mixture to a boil, then reduce the heat. Simmer, covered, stirring frequently, until the rice is tender, about 1 hour. Beat the eggs until light. Stir ¼ cup of the cooked rice mixture into the eggs, stirring quickly. Add the egg mixture back to rice mixture. Stir constantly over low heat until the pudding thickens, about 3 minutes. Remove from the heat. Cool before serving. Spoon the pudding into dessert dishes and garnish with cinnamon and whipped cream, if desired.

12 to 14 servings

Banana Bread

½ cup vegetable oil

1 cup sugar

2 large eggs

3 medium-size ripe bananas

1 cup buttermilk

1 teaspoon ground cinnamon

1 teaspoon vanilla extract

2½ cups all-purpose flour

1 teaspoon baking soda

½ teaspoon baking powder

¼ teaspoon salt

Preheat the oven to 325°F. Spray two 8 x 4 x 3-inch loaf pans with vegetable spray. Using an electric mixer, cream together the oil, sugar, and eggs on medium speed for 3 minutes. In a blender, puree the bananas with the buttermilk. Add to the oil mixture along with the cinnamon and vanilla. Stir together the flour, baking soda, baking powder, and salt. Gradually stir the flour mixture into the batter. Mix until smooth. Pour the batter evenly into the loaf pans. Bake until a toothpick inserted in the center comes out clean, about 45 to 50 minutes. Remove from the oven. Cool in the pans 15 minutes. Invert onto cooling racks to cool completely.

2 loaves

Variation. Add any of the following ingredients if desired:

½ cup chocolate chips

½ cup raisins or currants

½ cup chopped pecans

Strawberry Charlotte

2 envelopes unflavored gelatin

1 cup orange juice

4 large eggs

1½ cups milk

One 14-ounce can sweetened
    condensed milk

One 10-ounce package frozen
    strawberries in syrup, thawed

¼ cup strawberry preserves

2 tablespoons orange liqueur or
    orange juice

3 tablespoons cornstarch

¼ cup water

Three 4-ounce packages
    ladyfingers

1½ cups heavy cream

2 pints fresh strawberries

Whipped cream and fresh mint
    leaves for garnish

In a medium-size heavy saucepan, sprinkle the gelatin over the orange juice and heat until the gelatin dissolves. In a bowl, whisk together the egg yolks, milk, and condensed milk until well blended. Gradually whisk the egg-yolk mixture into the gelatin mixture. Cook over medium heat, stirring constantly, until the custard mixture thickens and coats a metal spoon, about 7 to 10 minutes. Pour into a bowl and refrigerate until the mixture is the consistency of unbeaten egg whites, about 45 minutes to 1 hour.

Meanwhile, in a blender or food processor puree the strawberries and preserves until smooth. Pour the mixture into a small saucepan. Stir in the orange liqueur or juice, cornstarch, and water. Cook and stir over medium-high heat until the mixture thickens and bubbles, then cook 1 minute more. Remove from the heat.

Line the bottom of a 10 x 3-inch springform pan with ladyfinger halves. Arrange a row of ladyfinger halves around the sides of the pan. Brush the ladyfingers with some of the thickened strawberry mixture. Cover the pan with plastic wrap and set aside.

When the custard mixture is thickened, beat the heavy cream on high speed with an electric mixer until stiff peaks form. Fold into the custard mixture. Spoon half the custard filling mixture over the ladyfingers on the bottom of the pan. Drop half the strawberry mixture by spoonfuls over the filling. Draw a table knife in a swirling motion through the custard and strawberry mixture to create a marbled design. Arrange another layer of ladyfingers over the filling, then spoon on the remaining custard filling. Repeat making dollops with the remaining strawberry mixture and marbling. Cover and refrigerate 6 hours or overnight. When set remove the sides of the pan. Transfer the charlotte to a pretty platter. Arrange fresh whole berries over the top and garnish with whipped cream and fresh mint leaves. Cut into wedges to serve.

16 servings

Mother's Day

Bruschetta

Herbed Roasted Chicken

Broccoli Puree

Stuffed Zucchini Flowers

Cheesecake

Frozen Raspberry Mousse

Herbed Roasted Chicken (page 60),
Stuffed Zucchini Flowers (page 62).
Striped plate by Cristina.

I'm blessed to have my grandmother with me still, so this day is always special. I celebrate by having Nony, Mom, and a few very close friends who are mothers over to my house, along with all the husbands and children, of course. Mothers

My mother, Renata Ferrare

have a special bond, and we use this day to reflect on our families and children. I think in particular about how blessed I am to be a mother, stepmother, and grandmother. Through our families we experience such power—the power of unconditional love that sustains us.

For this holiday I decorate with lots of flowers and children's art. I have the kids make place cards for their mothers—they draw on them and write special messages. And by each mother's plate is her Mother's Day gift. During the dinner I have the kids take Polaroids, and we put the pictures in frames to make keepsakes for the mothers.

The meal is as pretty as the table. The Herbed Roasted Chicken is always a favorite, whether it's for this special occasion or any time. The fresh herbs roasting on the chicken send a mouth-watering aroma through the entire house. The chicken comes out of the oven golden and crispy on the outside and moist and tender inside, and I strain the pan drippings and pour them over the carved pieces of chicken. The Stuffed Zucchini Flowers are a real treat, and add a pretty touch to the table.

Lunch starts at about one o'clock with a prayer of thanks, and I say a few special words to Mom and Nony. After everyone stops crying and hugging each other, we begin the meal!

Bruschetta

8 Roma (Italian plum) tomatoes,
   peeled, seeded, and chopped
¼ cup olive oil
8 garlic cloves, smashed
1 baguette, sliced into ½-inch
   thick slices

Chopped Italian parsley for
   garnish
Salt and freshly ground pepper
   to taste

To peel tomatoes, dip in boiling water for 1 minute, then immediately into cold water. Drain. The peel will come off easily.

Mix the tomatoes with the olive oil and garlic and marinate for a few hours. When ready to serve, remove the garlic and save for another use. Toast the baguette slices. Put tomatoes on top, sprinkle with parsley, salt, and pepper, and serve.

4 to 6 servings

Herbed Roasted Chicken

Marinade

1 cup Dijon mustard

1 cup olive oil

Juice of 4 lemons (reserve the juiced rinds)

½ cup soy sauce

2 garlic cloves, minced

Salt and freshly ground pepper to taste

One 5- to 6-pound chicken

4 sprigs of rosemary

4 sprigs of thyme

Whisk together the first six ingredients. Clean the chicken and marinate 4 to 6 hours or overnight.

Preheat the oven to 375°F. Stuff the chicken with the reserved juiced rinds and 2 sprigs each of rosemary and thyme. Roast the chicken in a covered roasting pan for 45 minutes or until juices run clear when chicken is cut at joint, then remove the lid and continue roasting, basting until golden brown.

Serve the chicken topped with remaining sprigs of rosemary and thyme.

4 servings

Broccoli Puree

1 pound fresh broccoli
One 8-ounce package nonfat or
    low-fat cream cheese,
    softened

2 tablespoons lemon juice
½ teaspoon ground nutmeg
Salt and freshly ground pepper
    to taste

Cut broccoli into florets. Steam or boil until tender, about 8 to 10 minutes. Drain well. In a food processor, combine the cooked broccoli, cream cheese, lemon juice, and nutmeg. Cover and puree until smooth. Season with salt and pepper. Serve hot or cold.

4 servings

Stuffed Zucchini Flowers

You can find zucchini flowers in specialty produce markets, Italian groceries, farmer's markets, or order them from your produce department manager.

2 Italian sausage links, cooked and crumbled

½ cup shredded Monterey Jack cheese

1 tablespoon grated or shredded Parmesan cheese

1 tablespoon chopped parsley

12 fresh zucchini flowers

½ cup all-purpose flour

Salt and freshly ground pepper to taste

2 large eggs, beaten

2 tablespoons olive oil

Lemon wedges for garnish

In a medium bowl, combine the sausage, cheeses, and parsley. Wash the flowers and pat dry. Carefully open the tops of the flowers and spoon about 1 tablespoon of the filling into each flower. If preparing ahead, cover the stuffed flowers and refrigerate for up to 2 hours before serving.

To cook the flowers, place the flour in a small bowl and gently combine salt and pepper. Place the beaten eggs in another bowl. Coat each flower first in flour mixture, then in the egg mixture, then in flour mixture again. Heat the oil in a large skillet. Sauté the flowers over medium-high heat for 3 to 4 minutes, turning to brown on all sides. Transfer the cooked flowers to paper towels to drain. Serve hot with a squeeze of lemon juice.

4 appetizer or side-dish servings

Cheesecake

Crust

1¼ cups graham cracker crumbs

¼ cup sugar

⅓ cup unsalted butter, melted

Filling

**Three 8-ounce packages cream
    cheese, softened**

1 cup sugar

3 large eggs

½ cup sour cream

2 tablespoons lemon juice

1 tablespoon vanilla extract

Topping

1 cup sour cream

3 tablespoons sugar

**2 cups any fresh berries
    for garnish**

Preheat the oven to 350°F.

For the crust. In a medium-size bowl, stir together the graham cracker crumbs, sugar, and butter until moistened. Press the crumbs into only the bottom of a 10 x 3-inch springform pan. Set aside.

For the filling. In a food processor, process the cream cheese and sugar together until smooth. (Or beat together on medium speed with an electric mixer.) Add the eggs one at a time, processing after each addition. Add the sour cream, lemon juice, and vanilla. Process until well blended. Pour the filling into the crust and spread evenly in the pan. Bake for 1 hour and 15 minutes, or until the top is set.

For the topping. Combine the sour cream and sugar. Spread the mixture over the cheesecake immediately after removing from the oven. Return the cake to oven for 5 minutes to set.

Cool the cake on a wire rack, then cover and chill thoroughly in the refrigerator. Just before serving, transfer the cake to a serving platter. Remove the pan sides. Top with berries.

16 servings

Frozen Raspberry Mousse

2 to 3 cups fresh raspberries
3 large eggs
1 cup sugar
Pinch of salt
1¾ cups heavy cream

Painting sauce
1½ cups fresh raspberries
2 tablespoons sugar
½ teaspoon lemon juice
Chocolate syrup or vanilla yogurt
for garnish

Puree the raspberries in a food processor. (Use more berries for a stronger raspberry flavor.) Strain out the seeds and set aside. In a medium-size bowl, whisk together the eggs, sugar, and salt. Place the bowl over a saucepan of simmering water and cook the mixture until it thickens and coats a metal spoon, stirring constantly, about 7 to 10 minutes. Cool mixture by placing the bowl in another bowl of ice water. Stir occasionally for about 5 to 10 minutes until cooled. Beat the cream on high speed with an electric mixer until soft peaks form. Stir the raspberry puree into the custard. Fold in the whipped cream. Pour the mixture into ten ½-cup molds or a 1½-quart freezer container. Freeze overnight or until firm.

For the painting sauce. In a blender or food processor, puree the raspberries with the sugar and lemon juice. Strain out the seeds. Drizzle the sauce on dessert plates. Unmold or scoop frozen mousse over sauce design. Garnish with drizzled-on chocolate syrup or stirred vanilla yogurt.

10 servings

Fourth of July

Barbecued Baby Back Ribs

Six-hour Best Baked Beans You'll Ever Eat

Easiest Barbecued Chicken in the World

Grilled Corn on the Cob

Potato Salad

Chopped Vegetable Salad

Pasta with Broccoli

Garden Greens with Raspberry Vinaigrette

Peach Pie

American Flag Cake

Fruit Punch

Barbecued Baby Back Ribs (page 69),
Easiest Barbecued Chicken in the World (page 71),
Grilled Corn on the Cob (page 71).

*F*or the Fourth of July, Tony and I invite family and close friends over to our house for an informal backyard buffet of traditional summer favorites. It's always important to me to set a beautiful, inviting table—even when paper plates and plastic cups are in order! So once again I decorate. I use red, white, and blue all over, and stick American flags everywhere—in the flower arrangements, in glasses, in the napkin rings, even in the food! We scatter tables all over the lawn, and I cover them with red tablecloths.

By July, the backyard garden is in full bloom. I get a great deal of pleasure (and, yes, energy) from working in my garden, and my kids take an active role in preparing the landscape and helping to choose the flowers and plants. My kids love to play chess, and I thought it would be fun (and a good way to keep them outdoors) if I built an outdoor-scale chess set. This turned out not to be difficult at all. I enlisted the help of Mayita Dinos, the gardening expert on my television show, Home & Family. We laid out red and white cinder blocks just like a real chessboard, and I found large chess pieces in the Hammacher-Schlemmer catalog. The kids love to challenge everyone to a game of chess, and it's a big hit on the Fourth of July.

We spend the entire day outdoors, except when it comes to serving the food. I set up the buffet in the dining room because I can't stand bugs. The minute you bring food outdoors, these flying things come at you from nowhere! But the day is a lot of fun, regardless. Around 6 P.M. we head down to the beach, where we watch a magnificent display of fireworks shot from a barge in the Pacific Ocean. Well-fed and pretty tired, we head back home, take the sleeping kids from the car, and put them to bed. They can take their baths in the morning!

Barbecued Baby Back Ribs

2 tablespoons olive oil

2 tablespoons (¼ stick) unsalted
   butter

1 cup finely chopped onions

4 garlic cloves, minced

2 cups catsup

1 cup red wine

¼ cup firmly packed dark
   brown sugar

2 tablespoons Dijon mustard

⅛ teaspoon cayenne pepper

2 tablespoons fresh lemon juice

1 tablespoon Worcestershire
   sauce

2 tablespoons grated lemon peel

Chicken stock or water, as
   needed

4 pounds baby back pork ribs

In a saucepan over medium heat, heat the olive oil and butter. Add the
onions and garlic and sauté until limp. Add the remaining ingredients
except chicken stock and ribs, in the order listed, and bring to a boil. Lower
the heat and simmer, uncovered, for 1 hour, stirring occasionally to prevent
sticking. Add chicken stock as necessary to achieve the desired consistency.
Keep the sauce warm or refrigerate for later use.

Preheat the oven to 300°F.

Place the ribs in a large pan and smother with the sauce. Bake,
covered, for 45 minutes. Remove the cover and cook 15 minutes more.
If possible, finish the ribs on the grill, basting with any sauce remaining
in the pan.

8 servings

Six-hour Best Baked Beans You'll Ever Eat

½ pound bacon

1 medium onion, chopped

Two 28-ounce cans baked beans, undrained

One 28-ounce can red kidney beans, rinsed and drained

1 cup firmly packed dark brown sugar

½ cup Dijon mustard

One 12-ounce jar chili sauce

½ cup catsup

Preheat the oven to 250°F.

Cook the bacon until crisp and drain on paper towels, then crumble. Reserve 2 tablespoons of the drippings in pan. Sauté the onion in the reserved drippings and drain. In a 3½- to 4-quart casserole or heavy pot, combine the baked beans, kidney beans, bacon, onion, brown sugar, mustard, chili sauce, and catsup. Cover and bake for 4 hours. Uncover and bake until the beans reach the desired consistency, about 1 to 1½ hours more.

15 to 18 servings

Easiest Barbecued Chicken in the World

Two 4- to 5-pound chickens, cut into serving-size pieces

4 cups of your favorite barbecue sauce

Preheat the oven to 350°F.

Toss the chicken pieces in the sauce and coat well. Place in a casserole dish and cover with foil. Bake for 1 hour. Remove the foil and continue to bake, basting frequently, until wonderfully golden. As the sauce breaks down, the natural sugars will make a thick, crusty gravy.

8 servings

Grilled Corn on the Cob

Fresh corn, husked
Unsalted butter

Salt and freshly ground pepper to taste

Place each ear of corn on a large square of aluminum foil. Top each with a pat of butter. Season with salt and pepper. Roll up the foil and fold the edges over to seal. Grill over medium-hot coals for 8 to 10 minutes, turning ears every minute. When you remove the foil you'll have tender, juicy corn!

Stovetop method. Place wrapped corn in a pot of boiling water for 10 minutes.

Potato Salad

Homemade mayonnaise
1 cup prepared mayonnaise
1 large egg yolk
3 tablespoons lemon juice
1 ½ cups olive oil
Salad
6 to 8 (4 ½ to 6 pounds) russet
   potatoes, peeled and cubed
1 cucumber, chopped
1 red bell pepper, chopped
6 scallions, chopped
2 celery stalks, chopped
½ cup green beans, cooked and
   diced
½ cup chopped parsley
2 tablespoons capers, drained
¼ cup Dijon mustard
2 tablespoons lemon juice
Salt and freshly ground pepper
   to taste
Lettuce leaves

For the homemade mayonnaise. In a blender or food processor combine the mayonnaise, egg yolk, and lemon juice. Process until blended. Through feed tube with machine running, add the oil in a thin stream. Process until the mixture is well blended. Set aside.

For the salad. Cook the potatoes in boiling salted water until tender. Rinse well with cool water and drain well. In a large bowl, combine the potatoes, cucumber, bell pepper, scallions, celery, green beans, parsley, and capers. In a small bowl, stir together 1 ¼ cups of the homemade mayonnaise with the mustard, lemon juice, salt, and pepper. Gently stir into the salad, mixing well. Spoon the salad mixture into a 10-cup mold and spread a thin layer of mayonnaise over the top. Cover and chill thoroughly. To serve, unmold the salad onto a lettuce-lined platter.

18 to 20 servings

Chopped Vegetable Salad

4 ounces green beans

1 ear white corn

½ cup diced white mushrooms

1 red bell pepper, diced

1 medium zucchini, diced

1 medium yellow squash, diced

1 large carrot, peeled and diced

2 Roma (Italian plum) tomatoes, diced

4 ounces Parmesan cheese, cut into small chunks

1 bunch arugula, chopped

2 cups mixed greens, chopped

Vinaigrette

2 tablespoons balsamic vinegar

2 tablespoons raspberry vinegar

2 tablespoons rice vinegar

1 tablespoon Dijon mustard

½ cup olive oil

Bring a large pot of salted water to a boil. Fill a large bowl with ice water. Plunge the green beans into the boiling water for 2 minutes, remove, and place in the ice water. When cool, place on paper towels to dry. Boil the corn for 2 minutes, remove, and place in the ice water. Cut the green beans into small pieces. Cut the corn off the cob. Combine all the ingredients and toss well.

For the vinaigrette. Combine all the ingredients and mix well. Add to the vegetable mixture and toss to mix well.

16 servings

Pasta with Broccoli

2 pounds fresh broccoli

1 pound bow tie (farfalle), shells,
   penne, or desired pasta

½ cup olive oil

8 garlic cloves, peeled and thinly
   sliced

⅓ cup lemon juice

1 teaspoon hot red pepper flakes

Lemon wedges

Trim off and discard the lower stems of the broccoli. Cut top of the broccoli into florets. Steam or cook in simmering water until crisp-tender, about 7 to 9 minutes. Drain and set aside. Cook the pasta in a large pot of boiling salted water according to the package directions until almost tender (al dente). Drain and rinse in cool water to stop the cooking. Set aside. In a small skillet, heat the olive oil and sauté the garlic with the red pepper flakes until the garlic is golden. Remove from the heat and stir in the lemon juice and red pepper flakes. In a large serving bowl, toss together the drained pasta and broccoli. Stir in the lemon juice. Pour the garlic mixture over the pasta. Toss well to combine. Serve chilled or at room temperature with lemon wedges.

6 to 8 side-dish servings

Garden Greens with Raspberry Vinaigrette

Raspberry vinaigrette
½ **cup olive oil**
⅔ **cup raspberry vinegar**
1 **teaspoon Dijon mustard**
1 **teaspoon sugar**

Salad
4 **cups mixed salad greens**
1 **cup fresh raspberries**
3 **ounces goat cheese, sliced**
  or crumbled

In a jar, combine the oil, vinegar, mustard, and sugar. Cover and shake well. In a salad bowl, toss together the salad greens, raspberries, and goat cheese. Shake dressing and pour over the salad. Toss and serve immediately.

4 servings

Peach Pie

Pastry for two-crust pie

2 cups all-purpose flour

1 teaspoon salt

½ cup butter-flavored vegetable
   shortening

6 to 7 tablespoons ice water

Filling

8 to 9 large ripe peaches, peeled
   and thinly sliced

1 cup sugar

¼ cup all-purpose flour

¼ cup quick-cooking tapioca

2 tablespoons lemon juice

2 teaspoons ground cinnamon

2 tablespoons milk

1 tablespoon sugar

For the pastry. In a bowl, stir together the flour and salt. Cut in the shortening using a pastry blender (I like to use my hands) until the mixture resembles coarse meal. Sprinkle cold water over the mixture 1 tablespoon at a time, stirring it in until the dough holds together. Shape the dough into a ball. Divide the dough in half and wrap each half in plastic wrap. Chill at least 1 hour or until ready to use.

Preheat the oven to 425°F.

For the filling. In a large bowl, combine the peaches, sugar, flour, tapioca, lemon juice, and cinnamon.

On a lightly floured surface, roll out half the dough from center to edge into a 12-inch circle. Wrap the pastry around the rolling pin and unroll into a 9-inch deep-dish pie plate. Ease the pastry into the pie plate without stretching it. Trim pie dough to ½ inch beyond the edge of the pie plate and fold under the excess pastry. Spoon the filling into the pastry. Roll out the remaining pie dough into another 12-inch round. Use a pastry wheel or ravioli cutter to make ¾-inch strips. Weave strips over filling to make a lattice crust, or a crisscross diamond pattern. (Or just lay half the strips one way over the pie and top with a second set of strips across them.) Press the ends of the strips into the edge of the crust. Fold the bottom pastry over the lattice strips, seal, and flute the edges. Brush the top of the pastry with milk and sprinkle with sugar. Bake for 15 minutes, then reduce the heat to 350°F. Continue baking until the fruit is tender and the pastry is golden brown, about 40 to 45 minutes more.

One 9-inch deep-dish pie

American Flag Cake

You can substitute three or four packages of ladyfingers for the pound cake.

One 3½-ounce package instant vanilla pudding

One 3½-ounce package instant chocolate pudding

4 cups milk

3 cups fresh strawberries

Two 10¾-ounce packages frozen pound cake, thawed

3 to 4 tablespoons rum or orange juice

Two 12-ounce containers frozen nondairy whipped topping, thawed

1 pint blueberries

Prepare the vanilla and chocolate puddings with the milk according to the package directions. Set aside. Slice 1 cup of the strawberries and halve the remaining 2 cups. Cut each pound cake into 16 slices. Line the bottom of a 13 x 9 x 2-inch baking dish with the cake slices. Sprinkle 1 to 2 tablespoons of rum or juice over the cake. Spread 2 cups of the whipped topping over cake. Sprinkle 1½ cups blueberries evenly over the cream layer. Arrange the sliced strawberries over the blueberry layer. Spoon 1 cup of the chocolate pudding over the fruit and spread carefully to cover. Top with another layer of cake slices and sprinkle with rum. Spread a layer of vanilla pudding over. (Cover and chill any remaining pudding for another dessert.) Spread the remaining whipped topping over the pudding layer. For the flag design, use the remaining ½ cup blueberries for the stars and the halved strawberries for the red stripes. Cover and chill until serving time. The cake can be prepared up to 24 hours ahead.

12 servings

Fruit Punch

One 32-ounce bottle Hawaiian Punch
Two 32-ounce bottles peach juice
One 1-liter bottle 7Up

1 pint peach sorbet
2 pints fresh strawberries, sliced
1 orange, thinly sliced
1 bunch fresh mint

Combine the juices and soda. Float the sorbet, strawberries, orange slices, and fresh mint on top.

Approximately 30 ½-cup servings

Late Summer Picnic

Spicy Buttermilk Fried Chicken

Pasta Pie with Sausage

Herbed Farfalle and Beef Salad

White Beans with Tuna Salad

Cherry Tomatoes with Feta and Basil

Italian Bread Salad (Panzanella)

Summer Zucchini Bread

Apple Pie

Pasta Pie with Sausage (page 85),
Italian Bread Salad (page 89).

*O*ne of my favorite memories of childhood is going to the lake for a summer picnic. Actually, it wasn't a lake, it was a quarry, but as far as I was concerned it was the ocean! It was so exciting to prepare our feast. Being Italian, our family and the other families would cook all day the day before to prepare for the picnic. We didn't have sandwiches; we had a banquet!

We would all pile into my dad's '56 Chevy, roll the windows down (it was always the hottest day in the history of the world), and count the minutes until we arrived. It took what seemed like forever to unload the car as we piled all the food, carefully wrapped in aluminum foil, onto the carefully shaded picnic tables.

I of course wanted to eat immediately, but no, we first had to go down by the water, put out our towels, rub Coppertone all over, and wait. While we waited, we sat there wearing these ridiculous-looking hats my mother had made for us out of napkins, so we wouldn't get sunstroke. She tied knots in all four corners and placed the napkins on our heads. They made us look like the Quaker Oats man. How humiliating! The only time we didn't have to wear these hats was in the water. So I would march to the water and stay there until I shriveled up like a prune while I waited for lunch. When it was finally time to eat, I would make a beeline for the table, only to be stopped by Mom and told that it was unhealthy to eat in a wet bathing suit. Who tells mothers these things?

So she and the other mothers would set up makeshift dressing rooms—really, just a towel strategically draped around us, with Mom protecting the open side with her body—so that we could change into dry clothes. God forbid she should drop it! The napkin hat was embarrassing enough.

Nice and dry, we finally dug in. It always tasted so good. We ate until we couldn't eat another bite and ran back toward the water, only to be told that we had to wait one hour before we could swim! It was the longest hour of my life.

Me in the pool as a kid with my sister and brother.

When I have a family picnic now, I always serve the food that reminds me of those happy times. But this tradition has evolved—I don't make my kids wait an hour after eating before they swim, and I know they wouldn't be caught dead in napkin hats!

Spicy Buttermilk Fried Chicken

2 cups buttermilk

¼ cup hot sauce

One 3- to 4-pound frying
   chicken, cut up, or 3 pounds
   chicken tenders

3 cups seasoned bread crumbs

1 teaspoon salt

½ teaspoon freshly ground
   pepper

3 large eggs, lightly beaten

Cooking oil

Pan gravy

½ yellow onion, chopped

1 cup chicken broth

2 tablespoons cornstarch

¼ cup water

Salt and freshly ground pepper
   to taste

In a large shallow dish, combine the buttermilk and hot sauce.
Add the chicken pieces. Cover and marinate in the refrigerator for 1 hour.

Preheat the oven to 375°F. Combine the bread crumbs, salt, and
pepper in a medium-size bowl. Place the beaten eggs in a shallow bowl. Dip
the chicken pieces first in the crumbs, then in the egg to coat. Dip in the
crumbs again until the chicken is well coated. Heat 2 inches of oil in a large
frying pan. Fry the chicken in hot oil until browned on all sides, but not
cooked through, turning often. Place the chicken in a shallow baking dish.
Bake until chicken is no longer pink in the center, about 20 to 30 minutes.

For the pan gravy. Pour off the oil from the pan, leaving the browned
bits. Add the onion and chicken broth, cooking until the onion is tender
and scraping the crusty bits off the bottom of the pan. Stir together the
cornstarch and water and stir into the pan. Bring the mixture to a boil, then
reduce heat. Cook and stir until the mixture is thickened and bubbly, then
cook 2 minutes more. Season with salt and pepper.

4 to 6 servings

Cristina Ferrare's Family Entertaining

Pasta Pie with Sausage

¼ *cup olive oil*

2 red onions, thinly sliced

¼ *cup firmly packed dark brown sugar*

1 pound linguine, cooked and drained

4 chicken sausages, cooked and cut up

1 cup shredded Monterey Jack cheese

1 cup crumbled feta cheese

6 large eggs

6 large egg whites

½ *cup grated Parmesan cheese*

First, caramelize the onions. In a large skillet, heat the oil, then add the onions and sugar and sauté over medium heat, stirring frequently, until the onions are very tender and browned, about 10 to 15 minutes. Drain and set aside.

Preheat the oven to 325°F. Spray a 10-inch cast-iron skillet or other heavy skillet with nonstick cooking spray.

Arrange one third of the drained linguine on the bottom of the pan. Sprinkle on half the cooked sausage, half the Monterey Jack and feta cheeses, and half the onions. Cover with another third of the pasta and remaining sausage, cheeses, and onions. Top with the remaining pasta. In a bowl whisk together the eggs and egg whites. Pour the eggs over the pasta and sprinkle with the Parmesan cheese. Bake until light golden brown, about 30 minutes. Let stand 5 minutes before cutting. Cut into wedges to serve.

6 to 8 servings

Herbed Farfalle and Beef Salad

This won me first prize in the Regis and Kathie Lee Celebrity Chef contest!

8 ounces farfalle (bow tie) pasta

⅓ cup olive oil

One 12-ounce New York strip
   steak

½ cup lemon juice

3 garlic cloves, minced

1 teaspoon cumin

½ teaspoon salt

¼ teaspoon freshly ground
   pepper

2 cups arugula or torn spinach
   leaves

½ cup cilantro

¼ cup chopped fresh basil

¼ cup torn mint leaves

2 tablespoons chopped parsley

Cook the pasta according to the package directions, drain, and set aside.

In a small skillet, heat 2 tablespoons of the olive oil over medium heat. Add the steak and cook about 4 minutes per side for medium doneness. Season to taste with salt and pepper. Remove from the pan and cut into slices.

In a large bowl, whisk together the remaining oil and the lemon juice, garlic, cumin, salt, and pepper. Add the arugula or spinach, herbs, steak, and pasta. Toss well. Serve at once or cover and chill up to 24 hours ahead.

4 main-dish or 8 side-dish servings

White Beans with Tuna Salad

1 pound dried white beans
    or four 16-ounce cans
    white beans, rinsed
    and drained
3 garlic cloves, peeled (if using
    dried beans)
Two 9¼-ounce cans water-
    packed white tuna,
    drained and flaked
1 bunch arugula, chopped,
    or 2 cups chopped fresh
    spinach

1 green bell pepper, chopped
1 red bell pepper, chopped
½ cup olive oil
3 tablespoons lemon juice
Salt and freshly ground pepper
    to taste
Lettuce leaves

If using dried beans. Place the beans in a 3-quart saucepan with enough water to cover the beans. Bring to a boil and boil 2 minutes. Remove from the heat, cover, and let stand 1 hour. Drain the beans and return them to the pan with fresh water to cover. Add the garlic. Bring to a boil, then reduce heat. Simmer, partially covered, until beans are tender, about 1 hour. Drain the beans and remove the garlic.

Place the beans in a large serving bowl. Add the tuna, arugula, peppers, olive oil, and lemon juice. Toss gently to mix. Season with salt and pepper. Serve at room temperature or cover and refrigerate up to 24 hours ahead. Serve on lettuce-lined plates.

6 servings

Cherry Tomatoes with Feta and Basil

Dressing
½ cup olive oil
2 tablespoons balsamic vinegar
3 tablespoons Dijon mustard
2 tablespoons lemon juice
Salad
4 pints cherry tomatoes
1 cup crumbled feta cheese

1 cucumber, peeled, seeded, and diced
½ cup chopped fresh basil
1 medium onion, sliced (optional)
Lettuce leaves

In a blender or food processor, combine the olive oil, vinegar, mustard, and lemon juice until well blended.

Discard the stems from the tomatoes and halve them. Place the tomatoes in a large serving bowl along with the cheese, cucumber, basil, and onion, if desired. Pour the dressing over and toss well. Serve immediately, or cover and refrigerate up to 24 hours before serving. Toss again before serving. Serve over lettuce leaves.

12 to 14 servings

Italian Bread Salad (Panzanella)

This is a variation on the classic Tuscan panzanella, which includes anchovies.

½ loaf 3-day-old Italian bread, cut into 1-inch-thick slices
½ cup cold water
¼ cup red wine vinegar
2 garlic cloves, minced
½ cup olive oil
Salt and freshly ground pepper to taste

1 medium cucumber, peeled, seeded, and cubed
5 large ripe tomatoes, cubed
1 small red onion, diced
½ cup fresh basil leaves, cut into thin strips

Sprinkle the bread with water and let stand for 2 minutes. Gently squeeze the bread dry and tear into 1-inch pieces. Spread the pieces out on a kitchen towel and let dry slightly.

In a small bowl, whisk together the vinegar, garlic, oil, salt, and pepper. In a large bowl, combine the bread, cucumber, tomatoes, onion, and basil. Add the vinaigrette and toss.

8 servings

Summer Zucchini Bread

3 large eggs

1½ cups sugar

1 cup vegetable oil

2 teaspoons vanilla extract

3 cups all-purpose flour

2 teaspoons ground cinnamon

1 teaspoon baking soda

¼ teaspoon baking powder

¼ teaspoon salt

2 cups shredded zucchini

1 cup chopped walnuts or pecans

Preheat the oven to 350°F. Spray two 8 x 4-inch loaf pans with cooking spray.

In a large bowl, beat the eggs until light and foamy. Beat in the sugar, oil, and vanilla. Mix lightly. Add the dry ingredients and blend well. Stir in the zucchini and nuts just until combined. Pour the batter evenly into the baking pans and bake until a toothpick inserted in the center comes out clean, about 45 to 55 minutes. Cool the loaves in the pans for 10 minutes, then remove from the pans and cool completely on a wire rack.

2 loaves

Apple Pie

Pastry for two-crust pie (see Peach Pie, page 76)

6 to 7 large green apples (such as Granny Smith, Golden Delicious, or any tart apple), peeled, cored, and sliced

½ to ¾ cup sugar

2 tablespoons all-purpose flour

1 tablespoon quick-cooking tapioca or all-purpose flour

2 teaspoons cinnamon

2 teaspoons lemon juice

1½ teaspoons grated lemon peel

1 tablespoon unsalted butter, cut up

1 tablespoon milk

1 tablespoon sugar

Prepare the pie crust as directed for a 9-inch deep-dish pie. Preheat oven to 425°F.

In a large bowl, toss together the apple slices, sugar, flour, tapioca, cinnamon, and lemon juice and peel. Turn the mixture into the prepared pie shell. Dot the filling with butter pieces. Place a second crust over the pie filling, fluting the edges as desired. Brush the crust with milk and sprinkle with sugar. Bake for 15 minutes, then reduce the oven temperature to 350°F. Bake until the apples are tender and the crust is golden brown, about 35 to 40 minutes more.

One 9-inch deep-dish pie

Thanksgiving

Crudités with Yogurt Curry Dip

Marinated Turkey with Chive Gravy

Extra Legs, Thighs, and Wings

Holiday Turkey Stuffing

Mashed Potatoes

Festive Glazed Yams

Sweet Potatoes

Spinach Puree

Orange-Walnut Cranberry Sauce

Last-minute Biscuits

Pumpkin Chiffon Pie

Blueberry Pie

Marinated Turkey with Extra Legs, Thighs,
*   and Wings (pages 97-98),*
Festive Glazed Yams (page 100),
Last-minute Biscuits (page 104),
Pumpkin Chiffon Pie (page 105).
Vegetable pottery vases (in background) by Cristina.

Thanksgiving is my favorite holiday. I love to prepare this meal, and the ambiance is just as important as the meal itself. I use Mother Nature to provide most of the decorations. The kids go out behind the house and collect leaves and twigs, and we make table decorations. If you have evergreens, cut some branches and use them as place mats, or put them in flower arrangements. It makes the house smell so good. I choose flowers in fall colors, and scoop out one large and several small pumpkins as containers for the flowers, and to hold votive candles.

This is how the week of planning shapes up. Monday, I do the grocery shopping, because it's not too crowded yet. Tuesday, I pick up the turkey as soon as the market opens to avoid the crowds. I also pick up extra turkey parts because I can't stand it when people fight over the wings and legs. That afternoon is devoted to setting and decorating the table. But first, I make a huge pot of homemade chicken soup. I do this for two reasons. First, we have a wonderful, hearty bowl of soup for dinner that evening. Second, I use chicken stock in my gravy to give it a full-bodied flavor. Wednesday is my cooking day—I do everything I possibly can in advance so that Thanksgiving Day will go smoothly.

I'm usually up very early on Thanksgiving morning. There's always a lot to do no matter how carefully I've planned everything. I start cooking the turkey around 11 A.M., and soon I have to maneuver among any number of people who have decided that the kitchen is the place to be. That's what I love about this holiday—family and friends, delicious aromas, great music. As the day goes on, I get more and more hungry "people pickers" in my kitchen, picking at everything before it's time to eat. When I bring out the turkey around 3:30 P.M. and let it sit before carving, they can hardly keep their hands off it! I do have some crudités for them to munch on—raw vegetables and a couple of great dips—which helps a little.

Once the turkey is carved, I call everyone to eat. I don't have to yell too loudly, because everyone is right there in the kitchen with me! We sit down to a wonderful, traditional meal, the flavors blending just so, nothing overpowering anything else. After we all have eaten our fill, a calm settles over the entire house. Everyone slows down, and we really start to talk and enjoy one another's company. Of course, tradition also demands that we complain about how much we ate, and say that the next day we're going on a diet until Christmas! Then someone asks, "When's dessert?" Around 7 P.M. I bring out the desserts, and they cover the entire table. All eyes are huge as they see this spread, and we indulge once again. I love this holiday!

Thanksgiving is really tiring!

Crudités with Yogurt Curry Dip

Yogurt curry dip

1 cup plain yogurt

1 cup low-fat sour cream

Juice of 1 lemon

1 teaspoon curry powder

1 tablespoon rum

¼ cup chopped fresh dill

Tabasco sauce to taste

Crudités

1 head broccoli, cut into florets

1 head cauliflower, cut into florets

4 large carrots, peeled and cut into 3 x ½ x ½-inch sticks

4 large cucumbers, peeled and cut into 3 x ½ x ½-inch sticks

Combine the dip ingredients and chill. Steam the broccoli and cauliflower florets for 2 minutes. Serve these or other favorites.

About 2¼ cups dip

Cristina's Famous Marinade

1 cup Dijon mustard

1 cup olive oil

¾ cup lemon juice

½ cup soy sauce

2 garlic cloves, minced

3 sprigs of fresh rosemary, chopped

3 sprigs of fresh thyme, chopped

¼ cup chopped fresh sage leaves

¼ cup chopped fresh oregano

In a 1½-quart bowl, whisk the ingredients until well blended. Use to marinate your choice of poultry, fish, or meat.

Approximately 3½ cups marinade

Marinated Turkey with Chive Gravy

One 20-pound fresh turkey

Salt and freshly ground pepper
to taste

Reserved lemon rinds from
marinade

Cristina's Famous Marinade
(see page 96)

3 sprigs of fresh rosemary,
chopped

3 sprigs of fresh thyme, chopped

¼ cup chopped fresh sage leaves

¼ cup chopped fresh oregano

Chive gravy

5 cups chicken broth or stock

¼ cup cornstarch

⅓ cup dry sherry

⅓ cup minced fresh chives

Salt and freshly ground pepper
to taste

Preheat the oven to 325°F.

Rinse the turkey and pat dry. Sprinkle with salt and pepper. Stuff the reserved lemon rinds into the cavity. Pull the neck skin to the back of the turkey and skewer closed. Tie the legs together. Twist the wing tips under the back. Place turkey breast side up on a rack in a large roasting pan. Pour the marinade over the turkey and sprinkle with the herbs. Cover with foil and roast for 2½ hours. Remove the foil and insert a meat thermometer in the thickest part of the breast or thigh, but not touching the bone. Continue roasting, uncovered, basting every 15 minutes, approximately 3 to 4 hours more, until the meat thermometer registers 185°F, a drumstick twists easily in its socket, and the turkey is golden brown. Remove the turkey from the oven and transfer to a carving board, reserving the pan drippings. Cover the bird with foil to keep warm. Let stand 15 minutes before carving.

For the gravy. Skim the fat from the pan drippings and transfer to a

(continued)

medium-size saucepan. Combine ½ cup of the chicken broth and the cornstarch and stir into the saucepan along with the remaining broth. If you want thicker gravy, repeat the process. Bring the mixture to a boil and reduce heat. Simmer until the mixture thickens and bubbles, then stir in the sherry and chives. Cook 2 minutes more. Season with salt and pepper. Serve the gravy with the turkey.

16 to 20 servings

Extra Legs, Thighs, and Wings

12 turkey wings
8 turkey legs
8 turkey thighs

Cristina's Famous Marinade
(page 96)

Preheat the oven to 325°F.

Arrange the turkey parts in a greased roasting pan. Pour the marinade over the turkey parts. Cover the pan with foil and roast for 1 hour. Uncover and continue roasting, basting every 15 minutes, for about 2 hours more, or until meat is golden and crunchy on top and no longer pink in the center.

About 20 servings

Cristina Ferrare's Family Entertaining

Holiday Turkey Stuffing

This recipe makes a lot of stuffing, but you can easily halve this version, using just one of the cans of soup, and halving all other ingredients. I use all the optional ingredients.

¼ cup olive oil

½ cup (1 stick) unsalted butter

2 medium yellow onions, chopped

1 bunch scallions, chopped

8 celery stalks, chopped

1 pound mushrooms, sliced

Two 16-ounce bags cornbread stuffing mix or bread stuffing

One 10¾-ounce can cream of mushroom soup

One 10¾-ounce can cream of celery soup

1 to 1½ cups chicken broth or stock

1 cup chopped parsley

½ cup orange juice

¼ cup lemon juice

Optional ingredients

1 cup chopped walnuts

6 Italian sausages, cooked and crumbled

1 cup chopped apple

1 cup raisins

Preheat the oven to 325°F.

In a large pot, heat the oil and butter. Sauté the onions, scallions, and celery until tender, about 10 minutes. Add the mushrooms and cook 2 minutes more. Transfer the mixture to a large mixing bowl. Stir in the remaining ingredients, moistening with more chicken broth as desired. Stir in any desired optional ingredients. Grease a large shallow roasting pan and turn stuffing into it. Cover with foil. Bake for 45 minutes. Remove the foil and bake until the stuffing is golden and crispy, about 15 minutes more.

About 30 servings

Mashed Potatoes

8 Idaho potatoes
½ cup (1 stick) unsalted butter
¾ cup milk

1 teaspoon salt
1 teaspoon freshly ground pepper
¼ cup chopped chives

Cut the potatoes in half but do not peel. Place the potatoes in a large saucepan with water to cover. Bring to a boil and cook until tender, about 25 minutes. Drain and gently pull off the skins. Mash with a potato masher or put through a ricer. Melt the butter in the milk and add to the hot potatoes ½ cup at a time. Keep mashing until smooth and fluffy. Stir in the chives and serve.

8 to 10 servings

Festive Glazed Yams

8 yams
¼ cup (½ stick) unsalted butter
1 teaspoon cinnamon

½ teaspoon vanilla extract
½ cup firmly packed dark brown sugar

Preheat the oven to 325°F.

Cut the unpeeled yams into thirds and cook in boiling salted water until tender. Drain, rinse under cool water, and peel. Place the yams in a greased shallow casserole dish. In a small saucepan melt butter, then stir in the cinnamon and vanilla. Pour over the yams and sprinkle with brown sugar. Bake until the syrup caramelizes, about 25 to 30 minutes.

14 to 16 servings

Sweet Potatoes

6 large sweet potatoes

2 tablespoons milk

¼ cup (½ stick) unsalted butter

1 teaspoon cinnamon

¼ teaspoon nutmeg

½ teaspoon salt

¼ teaspoon freshly ground pepper

One 10-ounce bag marshmallows

Preheat the oven to 325°F.

Cut the unpeeled potatoes into thirds and cook in boiling salted water until tender. Drain, rinse in cool water, and peel. Place in a food processor along with the milk, butter, and spices. Puree until smooth. (Or beat with an electric mixer or potato masher until mashed.) Spray a 2-quart soufflé or ovenproof casserole dish with cooking spray. Spoon in the potato mixture and cover the top with marshmallows. Make sure there is an inch of space at the top of the dish so that the marshmallows don't overflow during baking. Bake until the topping is golden and puffed, about 30 to 40 minutes.

12 to 14 servings

Spinach Puree

If you don't have time to wash and tear fresh spinach, use the convenient bagged, washed spinach available in your produce department.

3 bunches fresh spinach, washed and torn, or three 10-ounce bags washed, trimmed leaf spinach

3 cups water

3 tablespoons unsalted butter

3 tablespoons all-purpose flour

2 cups low-fat milk

1 teaspoon salt

½ teaspoon nutmeg

¾ cup grated Parmesan cheese

Preheat the oven to 325°F.

Place the spinach in a heavy stockpot with the water. Cover and cook until wilted, about 10 minutes. Drain well and rinse with cool water. When the spinach is cool enough to handle, squeeze out any excess liquid. Chop the spinach finely.

In a 3-quart saucepan, melt the butter and stir in the flour. Whisk in the milk and cook, stirring over medium-high heat until the mixture thickens and bubbles, about 5 minutes. Cook 2 minutes more. Stir in the salt and nutmeg, then stir in the spinach. Turn the mixture into a 1½-quart greased casserole dish. Sprinkle with grated Parmesan cheese. Bake for 30 minutes. If desired, brown the cheese under the broiler before serving.

About 10 servings

Orange-Walnut Cranberry Sauce

2 cups orange juice

2 cups sugar

Two 12-ounce bags fresh
    cranberries

Zest of 2 oranges

1 cup chopped walnuts

In a large saucepan, combine the orange juice, sugar, cranberries, and zest. Bring to a boil, reduce the heat to a simmer, and cook 10 minutes. Remove from the heat and cool before stirring in the walnuts. Refrigerate overnight before serving.

About 4 cups sauce

Last-minute Biscuits

2 cups all-purpose flour
1 tablespoon baking powder
1 tablespoon sugar
1 tablespoon crushed dried herbs
  (any combination such as
  basil, dill, fines herbes,
  rosemary, sage, or chervil)

¼ teaspoon salt
¼ cup vegetable shortening
¾ cup milk

Preheat the oven to 450°F.

In a large bowl, combine the flour, baking powder, sugar, desired herbs, and salt. With a pastry blender, or using two knives in a crisscross fashion, cut in the shortening until the mixture resembles coarse meal. Make a well in the center. Add the milk all at once and stir just until the dough clings together. Knead gently on a lightly floured surface for 10 to 12 strokes. Roll or pat the dough to a ½-inch thickness. Cut with a 2½- to 3-inch biscuit cutter, dipping the cutter in flour between cuts. Place the biscuits on an ungreased baking sheet. Bake until light golden brown, about 8 to 10 minutes. Serve hot.

16 to 18 biscuits

Pumpkin Chiffon Pie

1 envelope unflavored gelatin

½ cup sugar

½ teaspoon salt

½ teaspoon cinnamon

½ teaspoon allspice

¼ teaspoon ginger

½ teaspoon nutmeg

¾ cup milk

2 large egg yolks, beaten

1 cup canned pumpkin puree

2 large egg whites

¼ cup sugar

½ cup heavy cream, whipped

One 9-inch graham-cracker crust

Whipped cream for garnish

In a saucepan, combine the gelatin, sugar, salt, cinnamon, allspice, ginger, and nutmeg. Stir in the milk, egg yolks, and pumpkin. Cook over medium heat until the mixture bubbles and thickens. Remove from the heat and chill until partially set, about 1 hour.

Meanwhile, beat the egg whites until soft peaks form, then gradually add the sugar and continue beating until stiff peaks form. Fold into the pumpkin mixture along with the whipped cream. Pour into the pie crust and chill for 1 hour. Decorate the top with whipped cream rosettes.

One 9-inch pie

Blueberry Pie

Pastry for two-crust pie (see
   Peach Pie, page 76)

5 cups fresh blueberries, rinsed

1½ teaspoons grated lemon zest

2 teaspoons cinnamon

1 cup sugar

½ cup all-purpose flour

2 tablespoons quick-cooking
   tapioca

Vanilla ice cream or frozen
   yogurt

Preheat the oven to 400°F.

Roll out the pie crust and line a 9-inch deep-dish pie pan. Set aside.

In a large bowl, mix together the blueberries, lemon zest, cinnamon, and sugar. Add the flour and tapioca and mix again. Fill the prepared pie crust. Roll out a top crust as directed and put over the top. Trim the edges and cut steam vents in the top. Bake until the blueberries bubble and the crust turns a delicious golden color, about 45 minutes. Serve warm or cold with vanilla ice cream or frozen yogurt.

One 9-inch deep-dish pie

The Christmas Season

I always start my Christmas shopping in July! All over town the stores are having major sales. This is the time to find great buys. I do this for several reasons. The first is obvious: you save a lot of money. Second, around the holidays, it is next to impossible to find a parking space and someone who is in a good mood to help you. Third, I have a very large family to think about, not to mention the people who work with my husband and the people I work with on Home & Family. *I need to be organized so that I don't have a nervous breakdown! I want to be able to enjoy my favorite time of year.*

I keep a list of everything I buy, and for whom, along with how much I spend on each person. I keep the lists from year to year, so that I don't repeat gifts.

For any kids on my list, I include their ages and what kinds of things they like to do. When I bring home the gifts, I go directly to the Christmas closet, which holds all the wrapping paper and bows I bought at the day-after-Christmas sales. I wrap each gift, label it, and log it on my list with a little asterisk indicating that that person has been taken care of. With most of the gifts out of the way, I can easily deal with last-minute shopping for someone I've added to the list.

Now I can concentrate on what I love best—cooking! My fondest memories of Christmas are from when I was growing up in Cleveland. From Thanksgiving on, the house always had the aroma of freshly baked cookies, pies, and spice breads—everything gearing up to Christmas Eve dinner. Coming from an Italian background, it was the tradition to eat fish. We dined on linguine with calamari, scampi, clams, sea bass, and halibut, cooked in a delicate tomato-white wine sauce. Everywhere you looked, it was a feast for the table and a feast for the eyes. All the happy times with family and friends made an indelible impression on my life. This is a tradition I definitely want to uphold and pass on to my family.

I start preparing for Christmas the day after Thanksgiving. I want to make this special time last as long as I can. On Saturday, we all pile in the car and go pick out the most important feature to start celebrating—the tree! Too early, you say? Maybe, but if you take care of the tree properly, you will get it to stand tall until after New Year's Day. There are wonderful products on the market, such as Tree Green, Floral Life, and of course, good old-fashioned household remedies such as aspirin and 7Up. I put two aspirin tablets and a half-cup of 7Up at the bottom of the tree holder and fill it with water. Keep the pets from drinking it!

With most of the shopping out of the way, I can concentrate on planning the parties that go on all during the month. I pride myself in decorating the house with wonderful Christmas ornaments that I have collected over the years. It's so much fun to unwrap these little treasures and hear the children delight in remembering where we were when we bought them, or how they were made.

Christmas Tree Party

Oven-roasted Chicken with
Honey Dijon Glaze

Farfalle Pasta with Veggie-Meatballs

Caesar Salad with Homemade Croutons

Killer Brownies

Farfalle Pasta with Veggie-Meatballs (page 114).

This is family night! All our children come over to help decorate the tree. Everyone chips in. While the guys are unraveling the lights, the kids unwrap the ornaments and place them on the coffee table all in a row to make it easier when we put them on the tree. Usually the guys get pretty fed up with the lights and start to complain that dinner is taking too long. I usually make them wait until we get the lights on, or I'll lose them early!

We (actually I) decide what color lights to use, and whether they will twinkle, flash, or stay lit. We have had an all-blue tree and an all-red one, with huge red balls and big red ribbons—much to the dismay of Tony, who likes traditional all the way. He should have married Martha Stewart! We've had trees with huge white doves and twinkling white lights, and a tree with all hand-crafted ornaments and those bubble lights that look like candles—you know, the ones that make the tree look like it will catch fire any minute!

Christmas music in the background sets a nice holiday mood, and you can slowly feel the spirit of Christmas as the house comes alive with sounds and smells. Once I have secured the lights—and it's not easy, because I individually wrap each branch and the trunk—the effect is breathtaking. Then, after all this worthwhile effort, it's time to eat!

Alexandra and Arianna in front of the tree.

Oven-roasted Chicken with Honey Dijon Glaze

Glaze

1 cup Dijon mustard

½ cup olive oil

2 tablespoons honey

Juice of 4 lemons

½ cup soy sauce

2 garlic cloves, mashed

2 sprigs of rosemary

2 sprigs of thyme

**Salt and freshly ground pepper
   to taste**

16 chicken thighs, skinned

**½ cup parsley, chopped, for
   garnish**

1 lemon, sliced thin, for garnish

Whisk all the glaze ingredients together until well combined. Pour over the chicken and marinate for 2 to 3 hours in the refrigerator.

Preheat the oven to 350°F.

Roast, covered, for 40 minutes. Uncover and continue roasting, basting every 10 minutes until golden, about another 20 to 30 minutes. Remove chicken from roasting pan and put it on a platter. Drain the excess oil from the pan and add ½ cup hot water to the pan. Scrape the bits from the bottom of the pan and strain the liquid. Pour the strained liquid over the chicken and garnish with the parsley and lemon.

8 servings

Farfalle Pasta with Veggie-Meatballs

Sauce

1 carrot, chopped

1 celery stalk, chopped

½ cup chopped onion

½ medium zucchini, chopped

1 garlic clove, minced

2 tablespoons olive oil

1 pound lean ground beef

2 tablespoons white wine
   (optional)

One 15-ounce can tomato puree

¼ cup water

½ teaspoon salt

¼ teaspoon freshly ground
   pepper

Veggie-Meat Balls

1 Italian sausage, broken up

¼ cup grated Parmesan cheese

¼ cup catsup

2 tablespoons chopped parsley

1 tablespoon soy sauce

1¼ cups bread crumbs

2 slices white bread, torn into
   small pieces

½ cup water

1 teaspoon salt

¼ teaspoon freshly ground
   pepper

2 to 3 tablespoons olive oil

1 to 1½ pounds bow-tie or
   farfalle pasta

For the sauce. In a medium bowl, toss together the chopped carrot, celery, onion, zucchini, and garlic. Reserve 1 cup of the mixture and set aside. In a large skillet, heat the oil and sauté the remaining vegetables for 1 minute. Stir in ½ cup of the ground beef and sauté until no longer pink. Stir in the wine, if desired, tomato sauce, water, salt, and pepper and cook 1 minute. Remove from the heat.

For the veggie-meatballs. In another bowl, combine the remaining ground beef, sausage, and reserved vegetables. Stir in the Parmesan cheese, catsup, parsley, soy sauce, bread crumbs, bread, water, salt, and pepper.

Cristina Ferrare's Family Entertaining

Shape the mixture into small or medium meatballs. In a skillet, heat the oil and brown the meatballs on all sides. Add the meatballs to the sauce and bring to a gentle boil. Reduce the heat and simmer, partially covered, for 45 minutes. When the meatballs are ready, cook the pasta in a large pot of boiling salted water according to package directions. Drain. Pour the sauce over the pasta.

6 to 8 servings

Caesar Salad with Homemade Croutons

Homemade croutons
6 slices sourdough bread
½ cup olive oil
1 teaspoon garlic powder
Dressing
½ cup olive oil
1 heaping tablespoon yellow or
   Dijon mustard
2 anchovy fillets

Juice of 2 lemons
1 tablespoon Worcestershire
   sauce
1 garlic clove, smashed
2 heads romaine, washed and
   torn into bite-size pieces
½ cup freshly grated Parmesan
   cheese

For the homemade croutons. Preheat the oven to 350°F. Cut sourdough bread into bite-size pieces. Put them in a bowl and toss with the olive oil, then add the garlic powder and mix. Bake until golden and crunchy, about 10 to 15 minutes. Let cool to room temperature.

For the dressing and salad. In a blender, blend the olive oil and mustard. When the mustard has been incorporated into the oil, add the anchovies, lemon juice, and Worcestershire sauce. Blend, then pour into a glass jar or bowl. Add the garlic and let sit for at least an hour. Remove garlic. Pour over the greens and mix well. Add the cheese and mix again. Sprinkle with the croutons. Any extra dressing will last one week in the refrigerator.

8 servings

Killer Brownies

1 cup (2 sticks) unsalted butter

8 ounces (8 squares) bittersweet
    chocolate

3 ounces (3 squares)
    unsweetened chocolate

3 large eggs

1¼ cups sugar

1 tablespoon instant espresso
    powder

1 tablespoon vanilla extract

½ cup all-purpose flour

1½ teaspoons baking powder

½ teaspoon salt

1 cup chopped walnuts or pecans

6 ounces (1 cup) semisweet
    chocolate morsels

Preheat the oven to 350°F.

In a heavy saucepan over low heat, melt the butter and chocolates, stirring constantly, until smooth. Remove from the heat and let cool 10 minutes. In a large bowl, beat together the eggs, sugar, espresso powder, and vanilla with an electric mixer on medium speed until blended. Add the chocolate mixture and blend well. In a small bowl, combine flour, baking powder, and salt. Stir the flour mixture into the wet ingredients until well combined. Stir in the nuts and chocolate morsels. Pour the mixture into a greased 13 x 9 x 2-inch baking dish. Bake until the top appears dry, about 25 to 30 minutes (do not overbake). Cool completely before cutting into squares.

16 to 20 brownies

Kids' Christmas Party

Antipasto Salad

Spinach Salad

Chicken Cutlets

Ricotta-stuffed Shells

Macaroni and Cheese Casserole

Super Dooper Scoopers

Frozen Yogurt or Sorbet
(purchased from your favorite shop)

Super Dooper Scoopers (page 125).

The next party is the kids' party, for close friends and neighbors whose kids have grown up with ours. The kids really look forward to this party. It's always early in the season, usually the first week in December, and it keeps them in the holiday spirit all month long.

I involve the kids in the planning stages of the party. We start outside, and put out as many little twinkling white lights as we can. I always love to look at the children's faces as we step back and admire their work. Next, we sit down and figure out the menu. After we argue why we can't have Gummi Bears and M&Ms as our main course, we settle down to business. Pasta is a must! Luckily my kids love salads— one of their favorites is the spinach salad I've given here—so we fill the buffet with a variety, and a huge antipasto plate filled with Italian and Greek delights. (We do have grown-ups to think about, too.) We include wonderful ripened cheeses and fresh-baked breads, and for dessert we serve Super Dooper Scoopers that the kids make themselves.

The kids work the whole evening planning a show for us; they have been doing this since they were old enough to talk! We mothers sit and reminisce about previous Christmases, when the kids were still young enough for us to dress them in little velvet dresses and miniature suits and ties, as the men work overtime with their camcorders, getting the kids from every conceivable angle.

This show has the same basic elements every year, with traditional Christmas carols and a telling of the Nativity story. You can always count on the girls fighting over who gets to be Mary! As the kids get older, they bring some innovations to the program, creating some of their own material. It's wonderful to see the kids grow and change from year to year.

Antipasto Salad

3 large tomatoes, thinly sliced

1/4 pound Genoa salami, sliced

1/4 pound prosciutto, sliced

1/4 pound mortadella, sliced

1/4 pound provolone, sliced

1/4 pound mozzarella, sliced

1/4 pound fresh Parmesan cheese, cut into 1/4-inch cubes

1 cup Italian olives

Fresh basil leaves for garnish

On a large serving platter, arrange sliced tomatoes in two rows down the center. Arrange slices of meats and cheeses all around edge of platter. Sprinkle Parmesan cheese cubes over tomatoes; sprinkle olives over platter. Garnish with fresh basil leaves.

4 to 6 appetizer servings

Spinach Salad

8 slices bacon

2 tablespoons red wine vinegar

1 tablespoon Worcestershire sauce

1 bunch spinach, cleaned well and cut into julienne strips

2 large hard-boiled egg whites, crumbled

1/4 cup crumbled feta cheese

Cook the bacon until crisp and save the drippings. Crumble the bacon pieces and set aside.

In a small bowl, whisk together the vinegar, Worcestershire sauce, and bacon fat. Toss the spinach with the dressing. Garnish with the egg whites and feta cheese.

4 servings

Chicken Cutlets

8 skinless, boneless chicken
   breast halves
4 cups buttermilk
1 tablespoon soy sauce
1 tablespoon lemon juice
1 cup all-purpose flour
2 large eggs, beaten
2 cups seasoned bread crumbs

Salt and freshly ground pepper
   to taste
3 tablespoons olive oil
1 tablespoon unsalted butter
Juice of 2 lemons
1 lemon, sliced, for garnish
Chopped parsley for garnish

Pound the chicken breasts until thin and marinate in the buttermilk for 3 hours or overnight.

In a medium bowl, mix soy sauce and lemon juice into beaten eggs. Dredge each breast in the flour, shaking off any excess, then dip each breast in the egg mixture and let drain a bit. Coat with seasoned bread crumbs and then season with salt and pepper.

Heat the oil and butter in a large skillet over medium-high heat. Sauté the breasts until golden, about 2 minutes on each side. Squeeze lemon juice over each and serve on a platter with lemon slices and parsley.

8 servings

Ricotta-stuffed Shells

Sauce

12 Roma (Italian plum)
tomatoes, halved
1 bunch scallions, chopped
2 garlic cloves, minced
1 carrot, chopped
1 celery stalk, chopped
½ teaspoon salt
¼ teaspoon freshly ground
pepper
1 onion, chopped
½ cup olive oil
1 tablespoon unsalted butter

¼ cup dry white wine

Filling

24 jumbo shells or 12 manicotti
One 10-ounce package frozen
spinach, thawed
3 cups nonfat or low-fat ricotta
cheese
1 large egg white
½ teaspoon salt
½ teaspoon nutmeg
¼ teaspoon freshly ground
pepper
¼ cup grated Parmesan cheese

Preheat the oven to 325°F. Combine the first 7 ingredients in a 3-quart saucepan. Bring to a boil and reduce heat. Simmer, partially covered, for 45 minutes. Puree the sauce in a blender or food processor. Strain and set aside. Sauté onions in olive oil and butter until golden. Add white wine and simmer for 2 minutes. Add the sauce and cook for 10 to 15 minutes on low heat.

Cook the pasta in a large pot of boiling salted water according to the package directions. Drain, rinse in cool water, and pat dry.

Squeeze any excess liquid from the spinach and chop. In a large bowl, combine the ricotta, spinach, egg white, salt, nutmeg, and pepper. Using a pastry bag, fill the shells or manicotti with stuffing mixture and place them in a large oiled casserole. Pour the sauce over shells, then sprinkle with grated Parmesan. Cover and bake for 40 minutes. Uncover and bake 10 minutes more. Let stand 5 minutes before serving.

6 servings

Macaroni and Cheese Casserole

This rich, old-fashioned dish is very cheesy.

3 tablespoons unsalted butter

3 tablespoons all-purpose flour

2 cups milk, warmed

½ teaspoon salt

¼ teaspoon freshly ground
  pepper

1 pound (4 cups) shredded sharp
  cheddar cheese

1 pound (4 cups) shredded
  Monterey Jack cheese

1½ pounds elbow macaroni,
  cooked and drained

Preheat the oven to 350°F. Spray a 4-quart casserole dish with cooking spray.

In a small saucepan, melt the butter. Stir in the flour, then add the milk all at once. Cook and stir until the mixture begins to simmer, then reduce the heat and cook until smooth and slightly thickened and starting to bubble. Stir in salt and pepper. Stir in 3 cups each of the shredded cheddar and Monterey Jack cheeses until melted. Place the macaroni in a large bowl and pour the cheese mixture over it. Mix well and turn into the casserole dish. Sprinkle remaining cheese over the top. Bake, uncovered, until hot and bubbly, about 30 minutes.

18 servings. Recipe can be halved.

Note. This dish may be prepared ahead, covered, and refrigerated before baking. Bake within 24 hours, adding 15 to 20 minutes to the baking time.

Super Dooper Scoopers

Making these oversize cookies, and scooping the dough onto the cookie sheets, is a fun project for kids. The cookies must be slow-baked, or they will burn.

2¼ cups all-purpose flour
1 teaspoon baking soda
½ teaspoon salt
1 cup (2 sticks) unsalted butter, softened
¾ cup sugar
¾ cup firmly packed dark brown sugar

1 teaspoon vanilla extract
2 large eggs
3 cups semisweet chocolate morsels
1½ cups chopped pecans or walnuts
1 cup raisins

Preheat the oven to 275°F.

In a medium bowl, stir together the flour, baking soda, and salt. In a large bowl, beat the butter, sugars, and vanilla together with an electric mixer on medium speed until well blended. Beat in the eggs, one at a time, until well combined. Stir in the flour mixture until blended. Stir in the chocolate morsels, nuts, and raisins. With a medium-size ice-cream scooper or a large spoon, scoop the dough onto ungreased baking sheets, placing the mounds about 3 inches apart. Bake until the cookies are set and light golden brown, 35 to 40 minutes. Watch carefully to make sure cookies don't burn. Cool the cookies on racks.

Approximately 1 to 1½ dozen cookies

Grown-ups' Christmas Party

Wild Mushroom Risotto

Pomegranate Christmas Salad with
Holiday Vinaigrette

Cornish Game Hens with Stuffing

Chocolate Delirium Cake with
Chocolate Ganache

Wild Mushroom Risotto (page 130),
Cornish Game Hens with Stuffing (page 132).

*A*fter the wonderful chaos of the kids' party, it's time to throw a party for a few close adult friends and business associates. This party is one of my favorites! I usually hold it within a day or two of the kids' Christmas party, to take advantage of the decorations I already have up.

I start preparing for this party the first week in October. Everyone who comes to our home for this party leaves with a big basket filled with goodies from my kitchen—sauces, cookies and brownies, pastas, sautéed peppers, roasted eggplant, and wedges of Parmesan. I include a piece of homemade pottery as well. How do you make twelve to fifteen baskets and keep everything fresh? The secret, as always, is planning.

I start with the cookie dough, making one or two batches a day. I roll up the dough, wrap it in waxed paper, plastic wrap, and aluminum foil, and store it in the freezer. Then I start on the brownies. I bake at least two batches every day or every other day, depending on my mood, and seal them in an airtight container.

Next come the sauces. I don't start making them until December, and then I can usually do it over a weekend by cooking everything in volume. I make three different kinds: Fresh Roma Tomato Sauce I, Sausage and Pork Sauce, and Pesto. (Recipes appear on pages 206, 212, and 218.) After I prepare the red sauces, I fill Mason jars to one inch from the top, because the sauce expands as it freezes, label them with the date, and place them in the freezer. I put the pesto into Mason jars as well, and then fill the jars with an additional two inches of olive oil. This will keep the pesto from growing mold, and it will last a month in the refrigerator. Add new olive oil every time the pesto is used.

The menu for the dinner is of the utmost priority. Tony, for some reason, wants this to be a sit-down dinner, not a buffet. I need to figure out what will be the easiest foods for me to manage, since it kills me to think of paying a caterer. The thought of someone else in my kitchen drives me crazy, since I always feel I can cook the meal much better, and so much cheaper! I always start the meal with a pasta dish or risotto. It seems that everyone expects it when they come to our house.

I then turn my attention to the table settings. I make my own tablecloth—it's as easy as sewing material together in a straight line. Once the tablecloth is in place, I set the table, keeping in mind how many plates I'll need for the different courses. Over the years, I have managed to collect enough, but you can always rent or borrow what you need.

Use lots of candles—they really help set the mood by making the room look soft and warm. I make my own candles in the form of angels holding a page. After the wax has cooled, I paint them. Then I write the name of each guest in gold paint on the page, and use the candles as place cards. I've collected giant glass snowballs with beautiful Christmas scenes, and I scatter them around the table, along with pine cones, special ornaments, and yards and yards of gold beads that I intertwine through the flowers and ornaments.

To me, decorating a room is like painting on a canvas. Every detail is important, and every element helps complete the picture. It's always a showstopper when we enter the dining room and the only light in the room is provided by candles. The table looks as tantalizing as the food.

When our guests are ready to leave, I give each couple their Christmas basket. It's the nicest feeling in the world to give a gift filled with love. It makes me feel so good!

Now, totally exhausted, I give myself a break by going to other people's parties—realizing, of course, that Christmas Eve is coming up!

Wild Mushroom Risotto

1 small onion, chopped

¼ pound white mushrooms, thinly sliced

4 to 5 fresh shiitake or porcini mushrooms

¼ cup olive oil

2 cups Arborio rice

6 to 7 cups chicken stock

½ cup freshly grated Parmesan cheese

Zest of 1 lemon

¼ cup chopped Italian parsley

Salt and freshly ground pepper to taste

Sauté the onion and mushrooms in the oil over medium heat. Add the rice and stir to coat. In a large saucepan or pot, bring the stock to a simmer. Add 1 cup of stock to the rice mixture and stir until it is almost all absorbed. Continue adding stock ½ cup at a time, stirring well after each addition and allowing the stock to be mostly absorbed before adding more. You may need slightly more or less stock to achieve the desired consistency. When the rice is creamy but still firm to the bite and cooked through, add cheese, zest, parsley, salt, and pepper.

8 servings

Pomegranate Christmas Salad with Holiday Vinaigrette

Holiday vinaigrette

1 cup olive oil

Juice of 2 lemons

¼ cup rice vinegar

¼ cup balsamic vinegar

½ teaspoon sugar

¼ teaspoon salt

¼ teaspoon freshly ground pepper

1 garlic clove, smashed

1 pomegranate

2 bunches arugula

1 bunch red leaf lettuce

3 cups baby mixed greens or chopped romaine

1 cup crumbled feta cheese

Mix the first 7 ingredients in a glass jar, then add the garlic. Let sit for at least 1 hour or overnight. Remove the garlic. This will last 1 week in the refrigerator.

Cut the pomegranate in half and scoop out the seeds, making sure to discard the rind and membranes around the seeds. Set the seeds aside.

Put the greens in a large salad bowl. Add ½ cup of the vinaigrette and toss. Sprinkle the feta and pomegranate seeds on top.

8 servings

Cornish Game Hens
with Stuffing

4 Cornish game hens, cut in half

Marinade

1 cup Dijon mustard

½ cup olive oil

Juice of 4 lemons

½ cup soy sauce

2 garlic cloves, minced

*Salt and freshly ground pepper
    to taste*

*1 bunch each rosemary
    and thyme*

Stuffing

¼ cup olive oil

1 small yellow onion, minced

*1 Italian sausage, casing
    removed*

6 scallions, chopped

6 celery stalks, chopped

1 cup sliced white mushrooms

*8 shiitake mushrooms, thinly
    sliced*

¼ cup chopped Italian parsley

¼ cup white wine

6 cups sourdough bread cubes

1 to 2 cups chicken stock

Sauce

½ cup liquid (stock or water)

*1 tablespoon arrowroot or
    cornstarch*

*Parsley and lemon zest for
    garnish*

For the hens. Preheat the oven to 350°F.

Place the hens in a baking pan large enough to accommodate them in a single layer.

For the marinade. Combine all the ingredients for the marinade and pour over the hens, arranging the herbs on top. Roast, covered with foil, for 30 to 40 minutes. Remove the foil, baste, and place back in the oven continuing to roast until golden, about 30 minutes longer. Make sure to baste often. When cooked, remove from the oven and place the hens on a serving platter. Use baking pan for sauce below.

For the stuffing. In a large sauté pan, heat the oil over medium heat and add the onion and sausage. Sauté briefly, then add the scallions, celery, mushrooms, and parsley. Sauté until golden. Add wine and reduce the glaze, cooking about 1 minute. Cook until the vegetables are tender. Remove from the heat and place in a large bowl. Add the bread cubes and chicken stock and combine well. Place the stuffing in a 3-quart baking dish and cover with foil. Bake in the same oven with the game hens for 1 hour.

For the sauce. Place the baking pan over medium heat on the stove. Skim off the fat from remaining liquid in the pan. Turn up heat to high. Pour stock or water into a small bowl and add arrowroot. Mix together and then whisk into the pan to make a roux. Continue to whisk until sauce thickens to coat a spoon.

To serve, place a spoonful of stuffing on the plate and place a game hen half on top. Spoon the sauce over. Garnish with chopped parsley and lemon zest.

8 servings

Chocolate Delirium Cake with Chocolate Ganache

Prepare and glaze this cake at least 6 hours or up to one day ahead. This cake is incredibly rich and tastes like a chocolate truffle.

Cake

4 ounces (4 squares) semisweet chocolate

3 ounces (3 squares) unsweetened chocolate

6 tablespoons unsalted butter

¾ cup all-purpose flour

¾ teaspoon baking soda

Pinch of salt

5 large eggs

1 cup sugar

1 teaspoon vanilla extract

3 tablespoons sour cream

Chocolate ganache icing

1½ cups heavy cream

12 ounces (12 squares) semisweet chocolate

3 tablespoons unsalted butter

3 tablespoons sugar

Unsweetened whipped cream for garnish (optional)

Preheat the oven to 325°F. Butter and flour a 10 x 1½-inch springform pan.

For the cake. In a double boiler or a small heavy saucepan, melt the chocolate with the butter until smooth, stirring constantly. Remove from the heat. In a medium bowl stir together the flour, baking soda, and salt. Set aside. In a large bowl beat the eggs with the sugar and vanilla on low speed until blended, then beat on high speed until mixture is thickened, about 4 to 5 minutes. Beat in the melted chocolate mixture. By hand, fold in the flour mixture until blended. Stir in the sour cream. Pour the batter into the pan and bake until a toothpick inserted in the center of the cake comes out clean, about 40 to 50 minutes. Cool on a rack in the pan for 15 minutes, then remove the sides from the pan and cool completely. Carefully remove from the bottom of the pan after cooling.

For the icing. In a heavy saucepan, combine the cream, chocolate, butter, and sugar. Stir constantly over medium heat until the chocolate is melted and the mixture is smooth.

To assemble the cake, use a serrated knife to slice the cake horizontally into 3 equal layers. Set aside ¾ cup of the icing for the top of the cake. Place the top cake layer, cut side down, in the bottom of the same 10-inch springform pan. Spread half the remaining icing evenly to edges. Top with a second cake layer and spread with the remaining half of the icing. Cover and refrigerate for 30 minutes. Place a piece of waxed paper over a cooling rack and place the cake pan on it. Remove the pan sides. Pour the remaining icing over the top of the cake, spreading to cover the top and sides evenly.

Refrigerate, uncovered, for 2 to 3 hours, or until the icing is set. Transfer the cake to a serving plate and let stand 30 minutes at room temperature before serving. Slice into thin wedges. Serve with unsweetened whipped cream if desired.

12 to 16 servings

Christmas Eve Buffet

Mustard-glazed Salmon

Shrimp Scampi in Garlic White Wine Glaze

Seafood Salad

Octopus Salad

Red and Green Peppers in Olive Oil, Garlic, and Parsley

Mixed Baby Greens with Crumbled Blue Cheese

Assorted Imported Cheeses
(purchased from your favorite shop)

Raspberry-Pear Cobbler

Chocolate Brownie Pie

Mustard-glazed Salmon (page 139),
Seafood Salad (page 141).

I alternate each year, preparing Christmas Eve dinner one year and Christmas Day dinner the next. Christmas Eve is another extravaganza! This is when the whole family gets together for our traditional dinner. I call in the troops—Mom, Nony, and the kids all help out. It's an Italian tradition not to eat meat on Christmas Eve, so the buffet is filled with fresh seafood.

After we eat, we go to the living room to open presents. We started this tradition when I was little. We would drive our parents crazy until they agreed to let us open just one present. (We had to wait until morning for the other gifts, because Santa hadn't delivered them yet.) It was something all the children looked forward to after dinner. We opened our one present before dessert, otherwise we would have had to choke down those cookies!

With the kids occupied for the moment, we can enjoy our coffee and dessert and actually talk with one another. Before everyone leaves, my brother, Gino, brings out his guitar. We sing Christmas carols and reflect on what Christmas is all about.

When we have said our last good-byes, it's time for the kids to go to bed, which they do without incident. They race right up the stairs, hang up their clothes, brush their teeth, go to the bathroom, say their prayers, and go to bed, all without hitting each other. They don't need a glass of water. They don't need their feet rubbed. They don't get out of bed eleven times to tell us they can't go to sleep. I live for this night once a year!

Once they are tucked in their beds, Tony and I head for the Christmas closet! We pull out all the gifts for the children and start filling up their stockings. We finally get to bed and set the clock for six in the morning.

Mustard-glazed Salmon

If you like, have the person at the fresh fish counter remove the skin from the fillet.

1 tablespoon olive oil

2 to 4 tablespoons minced garlic

⅓ cup whole-grain Dijon mustard

¼ cup dry white wine

1 tablespoon lemon juice

One 2-pound salmon fillet, cut into 8 pieces

Additional olive oil

Salt and freshly ground pepper to taste

Lemon wedges for garnish

Preheat the broiler.

In a small saucepan over low heat, heat the oil and sauté the garlic in it until soft. Stir in the mustard, wine, and lemon juice until well combined. Remove from the heat. Arrange the salmon on an oiled broiler pan and rub lightly with olive oil. Season with salt and pepper. Broil for 2 minutes. Remove from the oven and brush the mustard mixture evenly over the salmon. Return to the oven and broil until the salmon is golden brown and cooked through, about 5 minutes. Serve with lemon wedges.

6 servings

Shrimp Scampi in Garlic White Wine Glaze

16 unshelled jumbo shrimp
(about 12 ounces)
2 tablespoons unsalted butter
2 tablespoons olive oil
4 scallions, chopped
6 to 8 garlic cloves, thinly sliced

½ cup dry white wine
¼ teaspoon freshly ground
pepper
⅓ cup chopped Italian parsley
Hot cooked pasta or rice

Rinse the shrimp and remove the shells up to the tail. Butterfly each with a small sharp knife by making a deep slit along the back from the head end to the tail, taking care not to cut all the way through the shrimp. Open the shrimp so they lie flat.

In a medium skillet over medium-high heat, heat the butter and olive oil, then add the scallions and garlic. Sauté briefly. Add the shrimp and cook for 1 minute on each side and stir the other ingredients frequently. Stir in the wine. Cover and cook until the shrimp are pink and opaque, about 1 minute. Stir in pepper. Sprinkle with parsley and serve immediately with pasta or rice.

3 to 4 servings

Seafood Salad

The ingredients are expensive, but this delicious salad is a wonderfully elegant dish for a holiday party.

Vinaigrette

1 cup olive oil

⅓ cup lemon juice

1½ tablespoons lime juice

2 tablespoons Dijon mustard

1 tablespoon soy sauce

4 garlic cloves, minced

¼ teaspoon coarsely ground pepper

Salt to taste

Salad

1 large whole lobster, cooked

16 medium shrimp, shelled, boiled, and sliced in half lengthwise

12 ounces crabmeat, cooked

1 cucumber, peeled, seeded, and chopped into ½-inch pieces

1 red bell pepper, seeded and chopped into ½-inch pieces

3 scallions, sliced (green part only)

1 avocado, chopped into ½-inch pieces

⅓ cup chopped parsley

Red leaf lettuce or arugula, fresh dill sprigs, and lemon wedges for garnish

For the vinaigrette. In a blender or food processor, combine the oil, juices, mustard, soy sauce, garlic, ground pepper and salt. Cover and process until well blended. Cover and refrigerate 1 hour to blend the flavors.

For the salad. Shell the lobster and cut the meat into bite-size pieces. In a large bowl, toss together the lobster, shrimp, crabmeat, cucumber, red pepper, scallions, avocado pieces, and parsley. Toss with the dressing. Line a serving platter with red leaf lettuce or a bed of arugula. Spoon the salad onto the platter and garnish with fresh dill and lemon wedges.

8 to 10 side-dish servings or 4 to 5 main-dish servings

Octopus Salad

2 pounds baby octopus, cleaned

1 dried red chile pepper

1 red bell pepper, diced

½ cup chopped Italian parsley

¼ cup chopped fresh basil

3 Roma (Italian plum) tomatoes, skinned, seeded, and diced

¼ cup chopped scallions

3 garlic cloves, minced

⅓ cup olive oil

Juice of 2 lemons

Salt and freshly ground pepper to taste

2 bunches arugula

Place the octopus in a large saucepan and cover with water. Add the chile, bring to a simmer, and cook until tender, about 20 to 30 minutes. Remove from the heat and drain. Let cool. Slice the octopus into bite-size pieces. Toss with the remaining ingredients except the arugula. The salad is best when allowed to marinate for a few hours or overnight. Serve on a bed of arugula.

8 servings

Red and Green Peppers in Olive Oil, Garlic, and Parsley

3 red bell peppers
2 green bell peppers
½ cup olive oil
6 garlic cloves, mashed

2 tablespoons chopped Italian parsley
1 teaspoon salt
1 teaspoon freshly ground pepper

Char the peppers under the broiler or on the stovetop, until black. Put them in a paper bag in the still hot but turned-off oven and turn the bag repeatedly for 5 minutes. Take the peppers out of the bag and peel the skin off under cold running water. Seed and cut the peppers into strips.

In a large sauté pan over medium heat, heat the olive oil, then add the garlic and sauté until golden. Remove the garlic, add the peppers, and sauté for 2 minutes on each side. Remove peppers onto a platter and sprinkle with parsley, salt, and pepper.

8 servings

Mixed Baby Greens with Crumbled Blue Cheese

Dressing
¼ cup olive oil
¼ cup walnut oil
½ cup white vinegar
Juice of ½ lemon
¼ teaspoon salt

Freshly ground pepper to taste

**1½ pounds mixed baby greens
of your choice**
¾ cup crumbled blue cheese
**1 cup cherry tomato halves
(optional)**

Combine all the dressing ingredients in a blender.

Place the greens in a large salad bowl, pour the salad dressing over and toss. Sprinkle on the blue cheese and garnish with cherry tomato halves, if desired.

8 servings

Raspberry-Pear Cobbler

Pastry crust

1 cup all-purpose flour

½ teaspoon salt

¼ cup butter-flavored vegetable
shortening

3 to 3½ tablespoons cold water

Filling

4 medium firm-ripe pears, peeled
and sliced (4 cups)

¾ cup sugar

2 tablespoons all-purpose flour

1½ cups fresh or frozen
loosepack raspberries, thawed

¼ cup (½ stick) unsalted butter,
chopped

Preheat the oven to 425°F.

For the pastry crust. In a bowl, stir together the flour and salt. Cut in the shortening using a pastry blender until mixture resembles coarse meal. Sprinkle cold water, 1 tablespoon at a time, over the mixture, stirring it in until the dough holds together. Shape into a ball and flatten. Place the dough on a lightly floured surface and roll to a 16 x 12-inch rectangle. Carefully transfer dough to an 11 x 7-inch baking dish, allowing the dough to overlap the edges of the dish.

For the filling. In a medium bowl, toss together the sliced pears, sugar, and flour. Turn the sliced pears into the baking dish and sprinkle the raspberries over. Dot with the butter. Turn the edges of the dough over the filling. Bake until the crust is golden brown and the filling is bubbly, about 45 to 50 minutes. Serve warm or cool.

6 servings

Chocolate Brownie Pie

Crust

¾ cup all-purpose flour

¾ cup (1½ sticks) unsalted
    butter, cut up

3 tablespoons firmly packed dark
    brown sugar

1 ounce (1 square) unsweetened
    chocolate, grated

4½ teaspoons evaporated milk

¾ teaspoon vanilla extract

Filling

3 ounces (3 squares)
    unsweetened chocolate

2 ounces (2 squares) semisweet
    chocolate

¾ cup (1½ sticks) unsalted
    butter, softened

1 cup plus 2 tablespoons sugar

1½ teaspoons vanilla extract

2 large eggs, lightly beaten

½ cup plus 1 tablespoon
    all-purpose flour

½ cup chopped pecans or
    walnuts

Berry salsa topping

1 cup sliced strawberries

1 cup raspberries

1 cup blueberries or blackberries

3 tablespoons sugar

1 to 2 tablespoons Grand
    Marnier or orange liqueur

Topping

1 cup firmly packed dark brown
    sugar

3 tablespoons heavy cream

2 tablespoons unsalted butter

1 teaspoon instant coffee

½ cup sifted powdered sugar

Vanilla ice cream

Preheat the oven to 350°F.

For the crust. Place the flour, butter, sugar, and chocolate into a food processor. Cover and process with on-off pulses until the mixture resembles coarse meal. Add the milk and vanilla and process again in on-off pulses until combined. Press the mixture into the bottom of a 9-inch pie plate and set aside.

For the filling. In a double boiler or heavy saucepan, melt the chocolate with the butter, stirring constantly. Remove from the heat and stir in the sugar and vanilla. Stir a small amount of the chocolate mixture into the beaten eggs, then return the egg mixture to the saucepan and stir until blended. Stir in the flour and nuts until well combined. Pour over the prepared crust and bake just until set, about 30 to 35 minutes. Cool in the pan on a wire rack.

For the berry salsa. In a small bowl, stir together the berries with the sugar and liqueur. Cover and let stand for up to 2 hours before serving, or chill to serve later.

For the topping. In a small saucepan over medium heat, combine the brown sugar, cream, and butter, stirring constantly, until mixture comes to a boil. Remove from the heat and stir in the coffee and powdered sugar, whisking until smooth.

When the pie is completely cool, spread the topping over the top of the pie. Let stand until set before serving, about 10 to 15 minutes, or cover and serve later. Serve cut into wedges with the berry salsa and vanilla ice cream spooned over.

One 9-inch pie

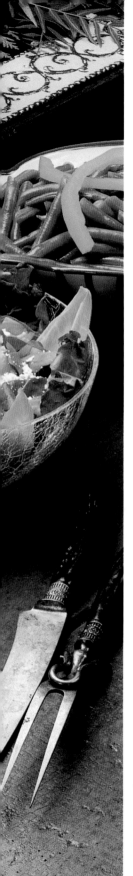

Christmas Day Dinner

Christmas Ham

Deep-dish Lasagna

French-style Green Beans in Dijon Vinaigrette

Sautéed Mustard Greens

Endive, Arugula, and Red Leaf Salad
with Feta

Orange-Walnut Cranberry Sauce
(recipe appears on page 103)

Assorted Breads
(purchased from your favorite shop)

Chocolate Bread Pudding

Christmas Trifle

Apple Cobbler

Thumbprints

Mexican Wedding Balls

Christmas Ham (page 151);
French-style Green Beans in Dijon Vinaigrette (page 153);
Endive, Arugula, and Red Leaf Salad with Feta (page 155);
Apple Cobbler (page 158).
Pie plate (pictured here with Apple Cobbler) by Cristina.

We like to be up before the children on Christmas morning, so we don't have to sit there blurry-eyed and with a full bladder. Been there! Tony and I go downstairs, turn on the Christmas tree lights, start the fire, and put on soft Christmas music. We get so excited when we hear little footsteps coming down the stairs, and we love the looks on their faces when they see the gifts for the first time. I pile the younger children's presents on each side of the fireplace, one side for Alex and the other for Ari, to keep them from throwing packages around in an effort to find theirs. Everyone else's gifts are under the tree. After the kids check out whether Santa ate the cookies and drank the milk, they open their gifts. Usually halfway through, our older kids arrive, this year with our new granddaughter, Claire. We exchange gifts, and then I go and prepare breakfast.

At 11 A.M. we go to a Christmas service at our church. It's so easy to get caught up in everything that's going on, and the beautiful Christmas service helps to remind us what this day is really about. When we get home again, we change into comfortable clothes, the kids play with their gifts, and the guys get frustrated because they can't figure out how to assemble the latest toys. It keeps them out of the kitchen!

When our whole family gets together there are twenty-five of us, and we always invite friends, so with such a crowd I let my guests bring their favorite dishes. I ask them to come around three o'clock for a four o'clock dinner, and when everyone starts to arrive, we just place the dishes on the buffet table or in the oven, and we're ready to go! I set the table with traditional pieces that I have collected over the years, and I light candles everywhere to give the room a warm glow. After dinner we all gather around the tree for Christmas carols. By that time I am happy, full, and totally exhausted. What a great feeling!

Christmas Ham

One 8-pound fully cooked smoked ham
About 40 whole cloves
½ cup orange juice
¼ cup Dijon mustard

1 cup firmly packed dark brown sugar
Honey-mustard sauce
1 cup whole-grain mustard
½ cup honey

Preheat the oven to 325°F.

With a sharp knife, score fat side of ham diagonally to create a diamond pattern, making cuts about ¼-inch deep. Insert whole cloves into the corners of the diamonds, all over top of ham. Place the ham, decorated side up, on a rack in a roasting pan. In a small bowl, whisk together the orange juice and Dijon mustard and pour over the ham. With the palms of your hands, pack the brown sugar over the top of the ham. Cover with foil and bake for 1 hour.

For the honey-mustard sauce. In a small bowl, whisk together the whole-grain mustard and honey until well blended. Cover and let stand at room temperature until serving time.

Remove the foil from the ham and continue baking until golden brown and crusty, basting the ham with the pan juices every 10 minutes for about 30 to 45 minutes. Cover and let stand for 10 to 15 minutes before slicing. Serve with honey-mustard sauce.

14 to 16 servings

Deep-dish Lasagna

Sauce
⅓ cup olive oil
1½ cup chopped onion
2 carrots, finely chopped
2 celery stalks, chopped
1½ pounds lean ground beef
2 Italian sausages, broken up
⅓ cup red wine
Two 29-ounce and one 14-ounce
   can tomato puree
Salt and freshly ground pepper
   to taste

Lasagna
One to two 16-ounce packages
   lasagna noodles (18-20
   noodles)
One 15-ounce and one 8-ounce
   container ricotta cheese
¾ cup freshly grated Parmesan
   cheese
Three 10-ounce packages frozen
   creamed spinach, thawed
2½ cups shredded Monterey Jack
   cheese

In a large skillet, heat the oil and sauté the onion, carrot, and celery until the onion is tender but not brown. Add the beef and sausage and cook until browned. Stir in the wine and reduce. Add the tomato puree. Bring to a slow boil, reduce the heat, cover, and simmer for 30 minutes. Season with salt and pepper.

Meanwhile, cook the noodles according to the package directions. Drain and rinse in cool water. Lay the noodles flat on a dry towel. Preheat the oven to 375°F. Spray an oversized or deep-dish lasagna pan with cooking spray.

To assemble the lasagna, spoon one quarter of the sauce over the bottom of the dish. Top with 4 to 5 noodles, one cup of the ricotta and ¼ cup of the Parmesan, and one package of spinach. Repeat the layers two more times. Top with noodles, remaining sauce, and Monterey Jack cheese. Cover and bake for 1¼ hours. Uncover and bake until lightly browned and bubbly on top, about 5-10 minutes more. Let stand 5 minutes before cutting.

French-style Green Beans in Dijon Vinaigrette

2 pounds green beans, sliced in half lengthwise
1 tablespoon Dijon mustard

Juice of 1 lemon
⅓ cup olive oil

Steam the beans, keeping them crisp. This will take about 5 minutes. Rinse beans in cold water.

Whisk together the mustard, lemon juice, and olive oil and pour over the green beans tossing to combine.

8 servings

Sautéed Mustard Greens

4 bunches mustard greens
½ cup olive oil
6 garlic cloves, sliced
1 teaspoon red bell pepper flakes

¼ teaspoon salt
½ cup raisins
Fresh lemon juice

Cook the greens in 3 cups water until wilted and soft. Drain well, squeeze out excess water, and chop.

In a large sauté pan over medium heat, heat the oil and lightly brown the garlic, then add the pepper flakes followed by the mustard greens, salt, and raisins. Sauté for 5 minutes. Squeeze a little lemon over it and serve.

8 servings

Endive, Arugula, and Red Leaf Salad with Feta

8 ounces red leaf lettuce

4 ounces arugula

8 heads Belgian endive,
   julienned

Dressing

½ cup olive oil

2 tablespoons soy sauce

2 tablespoons balsamic vinegar

Juice of 1 lemon

¼ teaspoon salt

½ cup crumbled feta cheese

Place the red leaf lettuce on platter in a pattern. Top with the arugula and endive.

Blend the dressing ingredients and pour over the salad. Top with the feta.

8 servings

Chocolate Bread Pudding

1 cup sugar

⅔ cup unsweetened cocoa
   powder

3 cups low-fat milk

2 large eggs

2 large egg whites

2 teaspoons vanilla extract

1 teaspoon ground cinnamon

⅛ teaspoon ground nutmeg

6 cups ½-inch bread cubes,
   crusts removed

Additional cocoa powder
   (optional)

Ice cream or yogurt (optional)

Preheat the oven to 350°F.

In a large saucepan over medium heat, stir together the sugar, cocoa, and milk until the cocoa dissolves. Cool for 10 minutes. In a large bowl, whisk together the eggs and egg whites. Stir ¼ cup of the cocoa mixture into the eggs, then stir in the remaining cocoa mixture. Stir in the vanilla and spices. Add the bread cubes and toss well to coat. Spray a 13 x 9 x 2-inch baking dish with cooking spray and dust with cocoa powder, if desired. Pour the bread mixture evenly in the dish. Bake until a knife inserted halfway between center and edge comes out clean, about 40 to 45 minutes. Serve warm with ice cream or yogurt, if desired. Refrigerate any leftovers.

8 servings

Variation. Substitute leftover cake or muffins for the bread cubes.

Christmas Trifle

Three 3-ounce packages
  ladyfingers
1/3 cup rum
One 4-serving-size package
  vanilla instant pudding mix
One 4-serving-size package
  chocolate instant pudding mix
4 cups milk

2 cups heavy cream
1/4 cup sugar
1 1/2 teaspoons vanilla extract
1 1/2 cups fresh strawberries,
  sliced
1 1/2 cups fresh raspberries
1 cup fresh blueberries
Mint sprigs for garnish (optional)

Split the ladyfingers and arrange them on a baking sheet. Brush with the rum and set aside. Prepare the vanilla and chocolate puddings, using the milk, according to package directions. With an electric mixer on high speed, beat the cream with the sugar and vanilla until stiff. Reserve ½ cup of the whipped cream mixture to garnish the top of the trifle. Cover and refrigerate until serving time. In a bowl, toss together the fresh berries.

To assemble the trifle, arrange a layer of ladyfingers in the bottom of a trifle bowl or large decorative glass bowl. Spoon half the chocolate pudding over the ladyfingers, spreading to cover. Top with another layer of ladyfingers and half the vanilla pudding. Top with a third layer of ladyfingers. Spread half the whipped cream over the ladyfinger layer. Sprinkle half the mixed berries over. Repeat layers with the remaining ladyfingers, pudding, and whipped cream. Sprinkle the remaining berries over the top of the trifle. Cover and refrigerate for at least 2 hours or up to 24 hours before serving. To serve, garnish with piped or spooned dollops of the reserved whipped cream and decorate with mint sprigs, if desired.

10 to 12 servings

Apple Cobbler

Cobbler

6 large Granny Smith apples,
peeled and sliced

1 tablespoon lemon juice

1 teaspoon vanilla extract

⅓ cup sugar

2 tablespoons quick-cooking
tapioca or all-purpose flour

1 tablespoon grated lemon peel

1 teaspoon ground cinnamon

½ teaspoon ground nutmeg

Pinch of salt

Streusel topping

⅓ cup sugar

¼ cup firmly packed dark brown
sugar

1 teaspoon ground cinnamon

⅓ cup cold unsalted butter,
cut up

Preheat the oven to 350°F. Spray a 12 x 8 x 2-inch baking dish with cooking spray.

For the cobbler. In a large bowl, toss together the apples, lemon juice, and vanilla. In a small bowl, stir together the sugar, tapioca, lemon peel, cinnamon, nutmeg, and salt. Add to the apple mixture and toss well. Turn the mixture into the baking dish.

For the streusel. In a food processor, combine the sugars and cinnamon. Add butter pieces and process with several on-off pulses just until the mixture is crumbly. (Or combine the ingredients in a mixing bowl and cut in the butter with a pastry blender until crumbly.) Sprinkle mixture evenly over the apples. Bake until the apples are tender, about 45 to 55 minutes. Cool on a rack. Serve warm or cool.

6 to 8 servings

Thumbprints

1 cup (2 sticks) unsalted butter,
  softened
1 cup sugar
2 large egg yolks
1 teaspoon vanilla extract
2⅔ cups sifted cake flour
2 teaspoons baking powder

1 teaspoon ground nutmeg
½ teaspoon salt
2 large egg whites, lightly beaten
2 cups finely chopped walnuts
  or pecans
½ cup of your favorite fruit
  preserves

Preheat the oven to 350°F.

In a large mixing bowl, cream the butter and sugar with an electric mixer set on high until fluffy. Beat in the egg yolks one at a time, then beat in the vanilla. In another bowl, stir together the cake flour, baking powder, nutmeg, and salt. Stir the dry ingredients into the butter mixture until well blended. With lightly floured hands, shape the dough into 1-inch balls. Dip each ball into beaten egg white and roll in chopped nuts to coat. Place 2 inches apart on ungreased baking sheets. With your thumb, make an indentation in the center of each ball and spoon ½ teaspoon preserves into the imprint. Bake until the cookies are set and a light golden brown, about 14 to 16 minutes.

Approximately 4 dozen cookies

Mexican Wedding Balls

1 cup (2 sticks) unsalted butter,
   softened
½ cup sugar
2 teaspoons vanilla extract
2 cups sifted cake flour

2 cups finely chopped pecans
   or walnuts
½ teaspoon salt
Powdered sugar

Preheat the oven to 350°F.

In a medium bowl, cream the butter, sugar, and vanilla with an electric mixer set on high until fluffy. In another bowl, stir together the flour, pecans, and salt. Stir the dry ingredients into the butter mixture until blended. Cover and chill the dough about 1 to 2 hours, or until stiff enough to shape. With lightly floured hands, roll the dough into 1-inch balls. Place on ungreased baking sheets and bake until light golden brown, about 12 to 15 minutes. Transfer the cookies to cooling racks and roll in powdered sugar while still warm. When the cookies are cool, roll again in powdered sugar.

Approximately 4 dozen cookies

Make Your Own Holiday

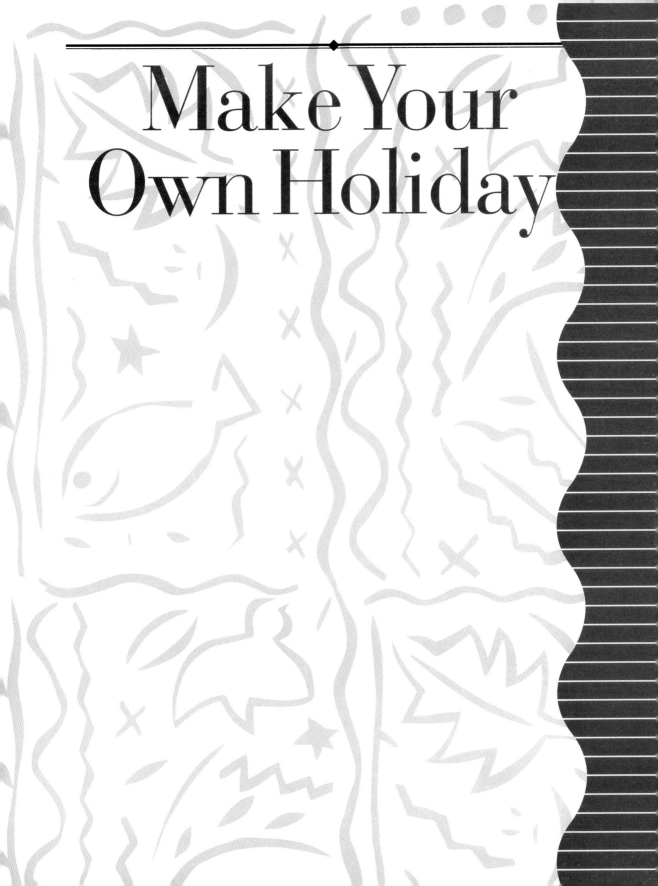

Girlfriend's Birthday Party

Arugula and Mixed Baby Greens

Pasta Primavera

Carrot Cake with Cream Cheese Icing

Pasta Primavera (page 166).

I have a few really close girlfriends—you know, the ones you can laugh with, cry with, share your innermost secrets with; the ones you can count on no matter what. These friendships should be nurtured and treasured. So when I give a birthday lunch, I go all out. I always serve food my friend likes—usually a light pasta dish and a salad, with carrot cake the only slightly decadent touch, since everyone's always on a diet.

Table set with keepsake plants.

I always decorate the table according to my friend's interests. I have one friend who loves angels, so I bring out beautiful ceramic angels that I made and use them as a centerpiece. I tie the napkins with a ribbon, and attach an angel ornament. Another friend loves books and writing, so I buy little gift books with lovely sayings, thoughts, and poems, and use them as party favors, along with little pads and pencils with which the guests can write something personal to the birthday girl. I also take some Polaroids of the guests and present the notes and photos to my friend, along with an album to keep them in. This is also a great idea for wedding and baby showers and other special occasions.

I also love to paint small vases, arrange my friend's favorite flowers or plants in them, and use them as place cards. Then, when the guests leave, they have a keepsake to take home with them.

Arugula and Mixed Baby Greens

Juice of 1 lemon

¼ cup olive oil

1 tablespoon rice wine vinegar

¼ teaspoon salt

2 bunches arugula

½ pound mixed baby greens

¼ cup chopped chives

Freshly ground or cracked
    pepper to taste

Whisk together the lemon juice, oil, rice wine vinegar, and salt. Place the remaining ingredients in a salad bowl and toss with dressing. Top with freshly ground or cracked pepper.

6 servings

Pasta Primavera

I mix the cream sauce in with the pasta and vegetables; the tomato sauce is spooned over each serving of pasta.

Cream sauce

2 garlic cloves

1 tablespoon olive oil

1 cup ricotta cheese

½ cup milk

¼ cup chopped fresh basil

½ teaspoon salt

¼ teaspoon freshly ground
   pepper

Tomato sauce

2 tablespoons olive oil

1 bunch scallions, sliced

4 garlic cloves, minced

4 large tomatoes or 12 Roma
   (Italian plum) tomatoes,
   skinned, seeded, and chopped

½ teaspoon salt

¼ teaspoon freshly ground
   pepper

Vegetables

1 bunch fresh asparagus

3 to 4 tablespoons olive oil

1 bunch scallions, sliced

4 garlic cloves, minced

2 medium zucchini, chopped

2 medium yellow squash,
   chopped

1 red bell pepper, chopped

1 cup broccoli florets

6 shiitake mushrooms, sliced

½ cup fresh peas

Freshly grated Parmesan cheese
   and fresh basil leaves
   for garnish

1½ pounds linguine

For the cream sauce. In a small skillet, sauté the garlic in the olive oil just until tender but not browned. Drain. In a blender or food processor, combine the ricotta, milk, garlic, basil, salt, and pepper. Cover and blend until smooth. Set aside.

For the tomato sauce. In a medium skillet, heat the olive oil and sauté the scallions and garlic until the garlic is tender but not brown. Stir in the tomatoes, salt, and pepper, then sauté for 10 minutes. Cover and keep warm while preparing the pasta and vegetables.

For the vegetables. Snap off the tough bottom ends of the asparagus, discarding the ends. Chop asparagus. Meanwhile, in a large skillet, heat the oil and sauté the scallions and garlic for 2 minutes. Stir in the asparagus and remaining vegetables. Cook until crisp-tender, about 8 to 10 minutes.

Cook the pasta in boiling salted water according to package directions until al dente and drain. Return the drained pasta to the pan, add the cooked vegetables and cream sauce, and toss well. Serve the pasta on heated serving plates. Top each serving with tomato sauce, Parmesan cheese, and basil leaves.

8 servings

Carrot Cake with Cream Cheese Icing

Indulge yourself with this dessert that is low fat, low fat, low fat.

Cake

4 large eggs

½ cup canola oil

¾ cup sugar

1 cup firmly packed dark brown
   sugar

½ cup low-fat buttermilk

2½ cups all-purpose flour

2 teaspoons baking soda

2 teaspoons baking powder

2 teaspoons ground cinnamon

½ teaspoon ground allspice

¼ teaspoon salt

3 cups shredded carrots

Cream cheese icing

One 8-ounce package fat-free
   cream cheese

One 16-ounce box powdered
   sugar

2 teaspoons vanilla

Preheat the oven to 350°F. Grease two 9 x 5-inch loaf pans.

For the cake. With an electric mixer set on low, beat together the eggs, oil, sugars, and buttermilk until blended. Stir in the flour, baking soda, baking powder, cinnamon, allspice, and salt. Stir in the carrots. Divide the batter evenly between the pans. Bake until a toothpick inserted in the center comes out clean, about 40 minutes. Remove from the oven and cool on a rack for 15 minutes before removing from the pans. Cool completely on a rack.

For the icing. In a food processor or in a mixing bowl using an electric mixer, combine all the ingredients until well blended. Spread icing over the cakes.

2 loaf cakes

Anniversary Dinner

Cream of Asparagus Soup

Bibb Lettuce with Walnut-Lemon Vinaigrette

Glazed Sea Bass with
Scallion Pancakes and Cucumber Salsa

Blueberry Cobbler

Ice Cream
(purchased from your favorite shop)

Bibb Lettuce with Walnut-Lemon
Vinaigrette (page 175),
Glazed Sea Bass with Scallion Pancakes
and Cucumber Salsa (page 176).

*W*hen our anniversary rolls around in April, Tony and I usually like to go out to dinner with our kids, but then we save the weekend nearest our anniversary just for us. We take Alex and Ari to my mom's for the weekend, and after the kids are safely tucked away I start to prepare for our special time together. Of course I have already given a lot of thought as to what will transpire. I always include a meal that I know he will enjoy, and I make the evening as beautiful and romantic as I can.

Actually, I fell in love with Tony while I was watching him eat. We were living in New York at the time. On one of our first dates we decided to stay in and have a home-cooked meal. We took a cab to my favorite store in the world, Balducci's, in Greenwich Village. They have everything there—great breads, produce, Italian meats and cheeses—you name it! On that day Tony was in charge of going to the deli section to pick out the cheeses and meats. I shopped for mussels and clams to make a pasta sauce, and tender baby lettuce and arugula for a light salad. When we were finished making our selections we jumped into a cab and headed back to his house.

I started preparing the pasta, and the aroma of fresh garlic, herbs, and olive oil quickly filled the house. Tony was busy making the antipasto. He was so excited as he walked me over to the kitchen table and sat me down to fix me what he called his "taste thrill." I watched as he tore off a piece of bread, cracking it open to reveal the soft, tender insides. He proceeded to place a slice of onion on top (I thought, Oh my God, is he going to try to kiss me after this?), anchovies (I'm scared now!), feta cheese, and a slice of tomato, and then he poured olive oil all over the top. I watched as he brought it to his mouth. I could hear

the crunching of the crusty bread and the
snap of the onion, and I could see the
olive oil sliding down his hand and
glistening on his lips. He ate it with
such gusto, and then he grabbed me
and kissed me, not even caring that the
onions and anchovies might be
offensive. I went crazy! I loved that he
was so thoroughly in the moment.

Our first Thanksgiving as a married couple.

To this day almost thirteen years later, we still eat like this, and
enjoy each other with as much passion and humor as when we first
started out.

Cream of Asparagus Soup

2 pounds fresh asparagus
1 large yellow onion, thinly sliced
2 to 3 tablespoons olive oil
4 cups chicken broth or stock
½ teaspoon ground nutmeg
½ teaspoon salt
¼ teaspoon freshly ground
   pepper

One 8-ounce package nonfat
   cream cheese, cut up
   and softened
Light sour cream and chopped
   chives for garnish

Snap off the tough bottom portion of the asparagus stalks and discard the ends. Chop the asparagus. In a large, deep skillet, sauté the asparagus and onion in the olive oil for 10 minutes. Stir in the broth or stock and bring the mixture to a boil. Reduce the heat, cover, and simmer until the asparagus is tender, about 10 minutes more. Stir in the nutmeg, salt, and pepper. Puree the mixture in batches with the cream cheese in a blender or food processor until smooth and creamy. Serve soup hot or chilled. Garnish each serving with a teaspoon of sour cream and a sprinkling of chives.

4 to 5 servings

Bibb Lettuce with Walnut-Lemon Vinaigrette

Bibb lettuce
2 tablespoons olive oil
2 tablespoons walnut oil
1 tablespoon apple cider vinegar
Juice of 1 lemon

2 tablespoons chopped walnuts
½ cup red bell pepper, cut into
  small diamonds
1 orange, peeled and thinly
  sliced

Arrange lettuce on each plate. Mix vinaigrette ingredients and pour over lettuce. Top with walnuts, red bell pepper and orange slices.

4 servings

Glazed Sea Bass with Scallion Pancakes and Cucumber Salsa

Scallion pancakes

1 cup low-fat milk

½ cup all-purpose flour

2 large eggs, lightly beaten

¼ cup thinly sliced scallions

2 tablespoons toasted
sesame seeds

1 teaspoon sesame oil

½ teaspoon salt

¼ teaspoon freshly ground
pepper

Cucumber salsa

1 cucumber, peeled, seeded, and
chopped

1½ teaspoons low-sodium soy
sauce

1 tablespoon rice wine vinegar

2 teaspoons chopped scallions

2 teaspoons chopped cilantro

Sea bass and sauce

Four 3-ounce sea bass fillets

½ cup all-purpose flour

¼ cup soy sauce

¼ cup mirin or 2 tablespoons dry
sherry mixed with ½ teaspoon
sugar

¼ cup sugar

2 tablespoons sake or white wine

2 tablespoons olive oil

For the pancakes and salsa. In a bowl, whisk together the milk, flour, and eggs until blended (the batter will be slightly lumpy). Cover and let stand at room temperature for 30 minutes. Meanwhile, prepare the cucumber salsa by stirring together all the ingredients. Cover and let stand at room temperature to blend the flavors.

Stir the scallions, sesame seeds, oil, salt, and pepper into the pancake batter. Spray a small nonstick skillet with cooking spray. Heat the skillet over medium heat. When the skillet is hot, pour ¼ cup of the batter into the pan, tilting to coat the bottom. Cook until bubbly on the surface and golden brown at the edges, about 1 minute. Turn and cook 1 minute more. Transfer to a plate. Separate each pancake with waxed paper. Repeat with the remaining batter to make 8 pancakes. Cover and keep warm.

For the sea bass. Cut each fillet in half and roll in flour to coat. In a medium nonstick skillet over low heat, stir together the soy sauce, mirin, sugar, and sake. Stir frequently until the sugar is completely dissolved. Pour the sauce into a small bowl. Set aside. In the same skillet, heat the olive oil until very hot. Sauté the sea bass for 2 minutes on each side until lightly browned. Reduce the heat to medium, then stir in the sauce mixture. Cook until the fish is cooked through, about 4 minutes more.

To assemble each serving. Place a piece of bass on half of a pancake and spoon a teaspoon of the sauce over the fish. Fold the pancake over the fish to make a half-moon shape, then fold the bottom of the pancake over to create a V-shaped bundle or roll into the traditional cylinder shape. Arrange 2 filled pancakes on each serving plate. Spoon the remaining sauce over the pancakes. Garnish each serving with spoonfuls of the salsa. Pass the remaining salsa with the fish.

4 servings

Blueberry Cobbler

6 cups fresh blueberries, washed
⅓ cup firmly packed dark brown
   sugar
2 tablespoons lemon juice
Grated peel of half a lemon

1 teaspoon ground cinnamon
¼ cup (½ stick) cold unsalted
   butter, cut up
2 cups fresh bread crumbs
Ice cream

Preheat the oven to 350°F. Spray an 8-inch-square baking dish or a
9-inch deep-dish pie plate with cooking spray.

In a large bowl, toss together the berries, sugar, lemon juice, lemon
peel, and cinnamon. Pour half the berry mixture into the baking dish. Using a
pastry blender or two knives in crisscross fashion, cut the butter into the
bread crumbs until fine. Sprinkle half the crumb mixture over the fruit. Top
with the remaining fruit mixture and sprinkle the remaining crumbs evenly
over the top. Bake until hot and bubbly and light golden brown on top, about
35 to 40 minutes. Serve with ice cream.

6 to 8 servings

Mexican Fiesta

Oven-baked Tortilla Chips
with Homemade Salsa and Guacamole

Chicken or Cheese Enchiladas

Tortilla Soup

Refried Black Beans

Taco Salad

Mango Sorbet with Fresh
Raspberry Sauce

Oven-baked Tortilla Chips with Homemade
Salsa and Guacamole (page 183),
Taco Salad (page 187).

*W*hen people come to our house, they expect an Italian feast, but you can't have pasta all the time! Every once in a while I get bored with cooking the same old things, and I like to vary the menu for close friends who have eaten at our house many times. At first people seem surprised and even disappointed that they aren't getting pasta, but they always leave the house satisfied!

A Mexican fiesta is a delicious change of pace. I have all the plates and place mats, and Tony makes the best margaritas! Even though I don't believe in appetizers, I make an exception for this night. I go crazy eating chips, salsa, and guacamole!

Oven-baked Tortilla Chips with Homemade Salsa and Guacamole

Homemade salsa
6 Roma (Italian plum) tomatoes, diced
½ medium yellow onion, diced
1 jalapeño pepper, seeds removed and minced
½ cup chopped fresh cilantro
¼ cup fresh lime juice
Salt and freshly ground pepper to taste

Homemade guacamole
2 to 3 ripe avocados
¼ teaspoon salt
1 teaspoon Tabasco sauce
Juice of 2 limes
½ cup homemade salsa

Two 9-ounce bags tortilla chips

Preheat the oven to 275°F.

Mix all the salsa ingredients together and set salsa aside.

Mash the avocados with a fork, then add the remaining guacamole ingredients. You can also puree all the ingredients in a food processor if you prefer.

Place the tortilla chips on an ungreased baking sheet and heat for 5 to 8 minutes. They will come out hot and crispy.

Place the salsa and guacamole in separate bowls. Place the tortilla chips in a basket or bowl. Arrange on a tray and serve.

6 servings

Chicken or Cheese Enchiladas

1 cup chopped onion

1 garlic clove, minced

2 tablespoons unsalted butter

One 16-ounce can chopped
   tomatoes

¼ cup canned green chiles,
   chopped

1 cup tomato sauce

1 teaspoon sugar

1 teaspoon ground cumin

½ teaspoon salt

½ teaspoon oregano

½ teaspoon dried basil

12 tortillas

2 cups shredded cooked chicken
   or Monterey Jack cheese,
   or 1 cup of each

2 cups grated Monterey Jack
   cheese

6 scallions, chopped

2 jalapeño peppers, seeded and
   sliced

½ cup chopped olives

½ cup chopped cilantro

½ cup light sour cream

Preheat the oven to 350°F.

In a large saucepan over medium heat, sauté the onion and garlic in the butter until tender. Add the next 8 ingredients. Bring to a boil, reduce the heat, and simmer for 20 minutes.

Dip each tortilla briefly in the sauce to soften. Place 2 tablespoons of chicken and/or cheese, 2 tablespoons of the grated cheese, and 1 teaspoon of scallions on each tortilla. Sprinkle some jalapeños, olives, and cilantro on each. Roll up and place seam-side down in a 9 x 13-inch dish. Blend the sour cream into the remaining sauce and pour over the tortillas. Sprinkle with the remaining cheese. Cover and bake for 40 minutes. To serve, sprinkle with additional chopped scallions, jalapeños, olives, and cilantro.

6 servings

Cristina Ferrare's Family Entertaining

Tortilla Soup

1 tablespoon olive oil

4 corn tortillas, cut into ¼-inch-
wide strips

½ cup chopped onion

4 garlic cloves, minced

1 jalapeño pepper, seeded and
chopped

One 16-ounce can diced
tomatoes with juice

1 tablespoon ground cumin

2½ quarts strained chicken stock
or unsalted canned chicken
broth

Salt and freshly ground pepper
to taste

Chopped avocado, shredded
cheddar cheese, chopped
cilantro, cooked and chopped
chicken breast, and additional
sautéed corn tortilla strips for
garnish

In a skillet, heat the oil and sauté the tortilla strips until slightly crisp.
In a food grinder or food processor, place the onion, garlic, and jalapeño
and process until ground. Stir into the tortilla mixture and sauté, stirring
frequently, for 10 minutes. Stir in the tomatoes and cumin. Bring the mixture
to a boil, then reduce the heat, cover, and simmer 15 minutes. Stir in the
chicken stock and simmer 10 minutes more. Season with salt and pepper.
Puree the soup in a food processor or blender in batches until smooth.
Serve topped with desired garnishes.

Twelve 1-cup servings

Refried Black Beans

1 pound dry black beans
Water
1 bunch scallions, sliced
¼ cup chopped cilantro
1½ teaspoons salt
½ teaspoon freshly ground
   pepper

¼ cup olive oil
1 medium yellow onion, chopped
4 garlic cloves, minced
Sliced scallions and cilantro
   sprigs for garnish

To cook the beans, place them in a heavy pot with enough water to cover by 2 inches. Bring to a boil and boil 2 minutes. Remove from the heat, cover, and let stand 1 hour. Drain and rinse the beans and return them to the pot along with the scallions, cilantro, and fresh water to cover. Bring to a boil, then reduce the heat. Cover and simmer until the beans are tender, about 45 minutes. Drain, reserving about 1½ cups of the bean liquid. Place the beans, reserved liquid, and salt and pepper in a food processor. Cover and process until pureed.

To fry the beans, heat the oil in a large skillet. Sauté the yellow onion and garlic until tender but not brown. Add the bean puree and sauté until heated through. Serve garnished with sliced scallions and cilantro, as a dip for tortilla chips.

5 cups dip

Taco Salad

Salad

1 head iceberg lettuce, shredded

1 head romaine, chopped

1 cup grated sharp cheddar cheese

1 cup grated Monterey Jack cheese

½ cup chopped cilantro

2 large tomatoes, skinned, seeded, and chopped

6 scallions, chopped

Ground meat mixture

1 pound ground beef, chicken, or turkey

1 tablespoon oil

2 tablespoons chili powder

2 teaspoons ground cumin

1 teaspoon garlic salt

1 teaspoon onion powder

Dressing

½ cup olive oil

Juice of 4 limes

¼ teaspoon salt

8 taco salad shells, flour tortillas, or crispy or soft corn torillas (optional)

Place all the salad ingredients in a large salad bowl.

In a medium-size sauté pan over medium heat, sauté the meat in the oil. When browned, add the remaining ingredients and sauté briefly. Drain the meat and set aside to cool. Blend the dressing ingredients well and stir the dressing into the salad. Mix the meat into the salad.

You can serve in warmed taco salad shells or warmed flour tortillas, or with crispy or soft corn tortillas. Or you can simply serve it as a salad.

8 servings

Mango Sorbet with Fresh Raspberry Sauce

2 cups fresh raspberries

2 to 3 tablespoons sugar

1 to 2 tablespoons orange juice

2 pints mango sorbet

In a blender or food processor, puree the raspberries with sugar to taste and the orange juice. Strain to remove the seeds. Serve over scoops of mango sorbet.

8 servings

Chinese Party

Spring Rolls

Chinese Chicken Soup

Sliced Cucumbers
with Sesame Rice Vinaigrette

Cristina's Stir-fry

Chinese Chicken Salad

Orange Sorbet
(purchased from your favorite shop)

Spring Rolls (page 193),
Chinese Chicken Salad (page 198).

I really enjoy Chinese-style cooking. In truth I actually cook this way more often than not, and my kids love it—especially stir-fried vegetables. I have several well-seasoned woks, and I use them often. When I occasionally prepare a sit-down dinner for friends, I go all out. Chinese cooking is a bit more time-consuming because you have to chop everything, but it's worth it!

I start the meal with Chinese Chicken Soup served in dome-lidded bowls, with wide porcelain spoons, along with homemade spring rolls. (I've collected a lot of Chinese dishes, chopsticks, and cooking utensils—not expensive, but pretty.) I have to be careful here, because the spring rolls are so delicious that everyone wants seconds and thirds, and then they're too full to eat anything else! Before I serve the next course I refresh the palate with cold, paper-thin slices of cucumber salad. For the main course I serve my stir-fry over rice or rice noodles or my favorite, angel hair pasta—sometimes I use shrimp instead of chicken—and my famous Chinese Chicken Salad. Sometimes I serve this whole menu buffet style and put everything out at once so that people can pick and choose.

I find that cooking this way is a lot of fun, and you can vary the menu by combining different foods. I combine Italian and Chinese all the time. I also enjoy the fact that because we live in California we have access to fresh organic produce all year round. It makes such a difference. But it still tastes great no matter what!

Spring Rolls

2 tablespoons olive oil

6 scallions, chopped

1 tablespoon grated fresh ginger

2 garlic cloves, minced

1 cup fresh bean sprouts

1 cup finely shredded carrot

1 cup sliced shiitake mushrooms

12 medium shrimp, peeled,
    cooked, and chopped

1/4 cup soy sauce

1 tablespoon water

1 tablespoon arrowroot or
    cornstarch

1/2 cup chopped parsley

18 to 20 egg-roll wrappers

1 large egg, lightly beaten

Dipping sauce

2 to 3 tablespoons dry mustard

3 tablespoons water

1/2 cup catsup

1/2 cup peanut oil

In a large skillet, heat the olive oil. Sauté the scallions, ginger, and garlic for 1 minute. Stir in the bean sprouts, carrot, mushrooms, and shrimp. Sauté for 1 minute. In a small bowl, stir together the soy sauce, water, and arrowroot, then stir into the shrimp mixture. Cook and stir until the mixture thickens and bubbles, then cook 1 minute more. Stir in the parsley and set aside. Position an egg-roll wrapper on a floured surface with a point facing you. Spoon 2 tablespoons of filling just below the center of the wrapper. Fold the bottom point over the filling and tuck it under the filling. Fold the side corners over, forming an envelope shape, then roll up. Brush the last corner with beaten egg and press firmly to seal.

For the dipping sauce. In a small bowl, stir together the mustard and water, then stir in the catsup. Blend well.

Heat the peanut oil in a heavy skillet. Brush off excess flour and panfry the rolls, turning frequently with tongs, until brown on all sides. Transfer to paper towels to drain. Serve with the dipping sauce.

18 to 20 spring rolls

Chinese Chicken Soup

Homemade chicken broth

One 3- to 3½-pound chicken,
   rinsed

2 medium onions, halved

6 carrots, peeled and halved

8 celery stalks with tops, halved

2 cups parsley sprigs

10 black peppercorns

2 teaspoons salt

Dumplings

Reserved cooked chicken or
   2 cooked chicken breasts,
   skinned, boned, and chopped

½ carrot, chopped

2 scallions, chopped

2 tablespoons chopped cilantro

1 tablespoon grated fresh ginger

3 tablespoons soy sauce

One 12-ounce package wonton
   skins (about 56 skins)

Blanched snow peas, matchstick
   carrots, chopped cilantro, and
   chopped scallions for garnish

For the broth. Place all the broth ingredients in a large stockpot with enough water to cover the chicken by 2 inches. Bring to a boil, then reduce the heat. Cover and simmer until the chicken nearly falls off bones, about 1¼ to 1½ hours. Remove the chicken and cool. Strain the vegetables from the broth and discard them. Chill the broth overnight in a covered container. Chop the chicken breast meat, cover, and chill for the dumplings. Refrigerate the other chicken meat for another use. The next day, skim any excess fat from the broth. Measure 3 quarts of broth to use for the soup.

For the dumplings. Place the chicken breast meat, carrot, scallions, cilantro, ginger, and soy sauce in a food processor or blender, cover, and blend until processed. To make each wonton, position one skin with the point toward you. Spoon 1 teaspoon of the filling just off center. Fold the bottom point over the filling and tuck it under the filling. Roll to cover the filling, leaving 1 inch unrolled at the top. Moisten the right and left corners with water, then bring the corners toward you over the filling and press together to seal. Repeat until all of the filling is used to make about 55 wontons. (Filled wontons can be covered and stored in the refrigerator up to 1 day before serving.)

For the soup. In a large stockpot, bring the chicken stock to a boil, then reduce the heat. Drop the dumplings into the simmering stock and cook for 1 minute. Ladle the soup into bowls and top with desired garnishes.

Twelve 1-cup servings

Note. You can substitute 3 quarts canned low-salt chicken broth and 2 cooked chicken breasts, skinned, boned, and finely chopped for the homemade broth and chicken.

Sliced Cucumbers with Sesame Rice Vinaigrette

3 cucumbers

½ cup rice vinegar

1 tablespoon low-sodium soy sauce

2 tablespoons sesame seeds, toasted

Cilantro for garnish

Peel the cucumbers and cut off the tips on both ends. Cut them in half and scoop out the seeds. With a sharp knife slice the cucumbers paper thin. Place in a medium bowl, add the vinegar and soy sauce and mix well.

To toast the sesame seeds. Put the sesame seeds in a cast-iron skillet over high heat and heat until they just start to turn golden. You must shake the pan constantly to prevent the seeds from burning. This will release their oils and make them taste so good.

Transfer cucumber mixture to six plates or bowls. Sprinkle the sesame seeds on top of each serving. Place a pinch of cilantro on top of each serving.

6 servings

Cristina's Stir-fry

For step 1

¼ cup soy sauce

Juice of 1 lemon

1 teaspoon sesame oil

2 skinless, boneless chicken
  breast halves, cubed

2 tablespoons cornstarch

For step 2

2 tablespoons olive oil

2 garlic cloves

1 red bell pepper, seeded and
  sliced

1 green bell pepper, seeded
  and sliced

4 scallions, sliced

½ cup sliced shiitake mushrooms

For step 3

2 tablespoons olive oil

1 teaspoon hot red pepper flakes

¼ cup cream sherry

¼ cup soy sauce

Cooked white rice

½ cup chopped cilantro for
  garnish

Toasted sesame seeds for garnish

Step 1. Combine the soy sauce, lemon juice, and sesame oil and pour over the chicken. Let the chicken marinate in sauce for 1 hour. Stir in the cornstarch and coat the chicken thoroughly. Set aside.

Step 2. In a wok, heat the olive oil until smoking, then add the garlic. Stir-fry lightly and remove the garlic. Add the red and green peppers, scallions, and mushrooms and stir-fry. When the peppers are cooked but still crispy, remove and set aside.

Step 3. In the same wok, heat the oil and add the chicken, stirring well. Add the red pepper flakes, sherry, and soy sauce, and cook until the chicken is done. Add vegetable mixture and toss well.

Serve over rice and garnish with cilantro and sesame seeds.

4 to 6 servings

Chinese Chicken Salad

Dressing

Juice of 2 limes

½ teaspoon sesame oil

½ cup olive oil

1 tablespoon soy sauce

¼ cup rice wine vinegar

1 tablespoon Dijon mustard

½ cup chopped cilantro

Salad

½ cup cherry tomato halves

½ cup shredded carrots

1 celery stalk, cut into ¼-inch slices

3 skinless, boneless chicken breast halves, cooked and cut into ½ x 2-inch strips

2 heads romaine, shredded

¼ cup chopped scallions

1 cup Chinese noodles

¼ cup sesame seeds, toasted

1 pound cooked angel hair pasta

Combine all the dressing ingredients. In a large bowl, toss all the salad ingredients together and then toss together with the dressing.

Put the pasta on a serving platter and top with the salad. Drizzle any extra dressing on top and serve.

6 servings

Cristina's Favorites

Ravioli and Pasta Sauces

Ravioli

Nony's Ravioli

Cristina's Spinach Ravioli

Pasta Sauces

Fresh Roma Tomato Sauce I, II, & III

Marinara

Hot and Spicy Tomato Sauce

Quick Pasta Sauce

Meatballs and Sauce

Sausage and Pork Sauce

Pork Rib Sauce

Tomato Sauce with Prosciutto and Baby Peas

Tomato Sauce with Sirloin

Clam Sauce

Cristina's Pesto

Anchovy Sauce

Nony's Ravioli (page 204),
Fresh Roma Tomato Sauce I (page 206).

*R*avioli are one of my favorite things to eat. These days people stuff them with so many unusual combinations, like pumpkin and lobster, or goat cheese and olives. Not for me—I like traditional fillings!

One of my fondest memories of growing up is making ravioli with my grandmother. She would make the dough by hand and roll it in the pasta machine until it was flat. Then she would put the filling in, seal a layer of dough on top, and cut it into tiny, perfect shapes that I thought looked like fluffy little pillows.

After Nony made the ravioli, it was my job to take a tray full of the morsels into my bedroom, where I would lay them out carefully on a white, floured tablecloth that was spread over my bed. I was to place them neatly so that they could dry out and be counted. Nony was never one for eating before dinner, so I was told not to eat any, but the filling was so luscious that of course I would pop a few into my mouth, chewing as fast as I could because if I delayed she would know I was up to something. It proved rather difficult to swallow fast, since the dough got stuck to the roof of my mouth. Having swallowed as rapidly as I could, I headed back to the kitchen, where I was promptly popped on the back of the head. How did she know? She brought me to the mirror, and I found out. All around my mouth and up my nose were dustings of flour. Yes, a flour mustache gave me away. Did that stop me? No way! The next time I tried it I stopped to check in the mirror and wiped off the flour. Couldn't resist!

But as wonderful as Nony's handmade ravioli dough is, I have substituted wonton skins in the recipe I include here, because making your own dough can be intimidating, time-consuming, and messy.

I think the ravioli come out light and delicate using the skins, and they are so easy you'll want to make them again and again.

I've included many of my favorite sauces here, which you can serve with your favorite pasta. But whatever kind of pasta you choose, make sure that it's a semolina pasta. It will say so on the front of the box. That way you will be sure it won't be sticky and glutinous. There's no need to rinse the pasta after cooking it. Just be sure to cook it in lots of salted water.

Nony's Ravioli

½ *pound lean ground beef*

½ *pound ground veal*

½ *pound ground pork*

One 10-ounce package creamed
  spinach, thawed

1½ *cups ricotta cheese*

⅓ *cup grated Parmesan cheese*

1 large egg

1 teaspoon ground nutmeg

1 teaspoon salt

¼ *teaspoon freshly ground*
  pepper

Four 12-ounce packages square
  or round wonton skins
  (approximately 56 skins per
  package)

One of the tomato sauces
  in this section

Fresh basil leaves for garnish

In a skillet, brown the beef, veal, and pork and drain off excess fat. Transfer the meat to a large bowl and stir in the creamed spinach, ricotta cheese, Parmesan cheese, egg, nutmeg, salt, and pepper. Mix well. Line a baking sheet with waxed paper and spray the paper with cooking spray.

To fill the ravioli, place a wonton skin on a work surface lightly sprinkled with cornstarch or flour. Spoon a rounded teaspoon of filling in the center and brush the edges with water. Top with a second skin and press the edges together with your fingertips. Place the filled ravioli on the baking sheet. Repeat with the remaining filling and wonton skins to make about 80 to 90 ravioli. To stack layers of ravioli, sprinkle cornstarch or flour over each layer and cover with sprayed waxed paper. (To prepare ahead, cover the filled ravioli with plastic wrap and refrigerate up to 24 hours before cooking.)

To cook the ravioli, place into simmering salted water 6 at a time and cook 1 to 2 minutes. Ravioli will be translucent. Do not overcook. Remove carefully with a slotted spoon, drain very well, and serve with tomato sauce. Garnish with basil. Allow about 6 ravioli per serving.

14 to 15 servings

Cristina's Spinach Ravioli

2 pounds part-skim ricotta cheese

One 10-ounce package frozen creamed spinach, thawed

½ cup grated Parmesan cheese

1 teaspoon ground nutmeg

1½ teaspoons salt

¼ teaspoon freshly ground pepper

Three 12-ounce packages square or round wonton skins (approximately 56 skins per package)

One of the tomato sauces in this section

Fresh basil leaves for garnish

In a large bowl, stir together the ricotta cheese, spinach, Parmesan, nutmeg, salt, and pepper until well combined. Line a baking sheet with waxed paper and spray the paper with cooking spray.

To fill the ravioli, place a wonton skin on a work surface lightly sprinkled with cornstarch or flour. Spoon a rounded teaspoon of filling in the center and brush the edges with water. Top with a second skin and press the edges together with your fingertips. Place the filled ravioli on the baking sheet. Repeat with the remaining filling and wonton skins to make about 70 ravioli. To stack layers of ravioli, sprinkle cornstarch or flour over each layer and cover with sprayed waxed paper. (To prepare ahead, cover the filled ravioli with plastic wrap and refrigerate up to 24 hours before cooking.)

To cook the ravioli, place into simmering salted water 6 at a time and cook 1 to 2 minutes. Ravioli will be translucent. Do not overcook. Remove carefully with a slotted spoon, drain very well, and serve with tomato sauce. Garnish with basil. Allow 6-7 ravioli per serving.

Approximately 10 servings

Fresh Roma Tomato Sauce I

24 Roma (Italian plum)
   tomatoes (about 3¼ pounds)
1 cup thinly sliced fresh basil
   leaves
½ cup extra virgin olive oil

6 garlic cloves, minced
1 teaspoon salt
1 teaspoon freshly ground pepper
½ cup freshly grated Parmesan
   or Romano cheese

To prepare the tomatoes, plunge them into boiling water for 1 minute, then immediately into cold water. Drain. Strip off the skins and core. Halve the tomatoes, then scoop out and discard the seeds. Dice and place in a nonmetallic bowl. Stir in the basil, oil, garlic, salt, pepper, and Parmesan or Romano cheese. Cover and let stand at room temperature for 2 or 3 hours to blend the flavors, or cover and refrigerate up to 48 hours ahead. Serve at room temperature, or heat until warmed through. Ladle over your favorite hot cooked pasta or ravioli and toss well.

5 to 6 servings

Fresh Roma Tomato Sauce II

I like this sauce for my ravioli. It makes the dish so light!

¼ *cup extra virgin olive oil*

1 *medium onion, diced*

8 *scallions, chopped*

4 *garlic cloves, minced*

½ *cup dry white wine*

16 *Roma (Italian plum)*
  tomatoes, quartered (about
  2¼ pounds)

¼ *teaspoon salt*

1 *tablespoon unsalted butter*
  (optional)

In a large skillet, heat the oil and sauté the onion, scallions, and garlic until golden. Stir in the wine and simmer until the liquid is reduced by half, about 3 minutes. Add the tomatoes and salt and simmer, partially covered, for 20 minutes. Process the sauce in batches in a blender or food processor until smooth. Strain to remove seeds and skins. Stir in the butter, if desired.

4 to 5 servings

Fresh Roma Tomato Sauce III

4 tablespoons olive oil

24 Roma (Italian plum) tomatoes (about 3¼ pounds), quartered

2 carrots, coarsely chopped

2 celery stalks, coarsely chopped

1 medium onion, quartered

2 tablespoons unsalted butter

1 medium onion, finely chopped

½ cup dry white wine

1 teaspoon salt

¼ teaspoon freshly ground pepper

In a deep skillet, heat 2 tablespoons of the oil and sauté the tomatoes, carrots, celery, and quartered onion. Partially cover and continue to cook, stirring frequently, until the vegetables are tender, about 30 minutes. Transfer the mixture to a blender or food processor, cover, and process until smooth. Strain to remove seeds and skins.

In same skillet, melt the butter in the remaining olive oil. Add the chopped onion and sauté until tender. Stir in the wine and simmer 3 minutes. Stir in the pureed tomato mixture, salt, and pepper. Simmer, partially covered, for 45 minutes.

10 servings

Marinara

2 tablespoons olive oil
6 garlic cloves, minced
Two 28-ounce cans diced
  tomatoes in juice

¼ teaspoon hot red pepper flakes
¼ teaspoon salt

In a large skillet, heat the olive oil and sauté the garlic carefully until golden (do not allow it to burn). Stir in the tomatoes and their liquid, red pepper flakes, and salt. Bring to a boil, then reduce the heat. Simmer, partially covered, for 1 hour.

6 servings

Hot and Spicy Tomato Sauce

1 tablespoon olive oil
2 garlic cloves, minced
1 anchovy fillet, chopped
  (optional)
One 28-ounce can diced
  tomatoes in juice

1 to 2 teaspoons hot red pepper
  flakes
One 4-ounce can chopped ripe
  olives, drained
1 tablespoon capers, drained

In a large skillet, heat the oil and sauté the garlic and anchovy until the garlic is golden. Stir in the tomatoes with their liquid and red pepper flakes to taste. Bring to a boil, reduce the heat, and simmer, partially covered, for 40 minutes. Remove from the heat and stir in the olives and capers.

4 servings

Quick Pasta Sauce

1 medium yellow onion,
   quartered

2 carrots, quartered

2 celery stalks, quartered

4 ounces salt pork, cubed

2 tablespoons olive oil

½ cup dry red wine

Two 29-ounce cans tomato puree

One 6-ounce can tomato paste

1 teaspoon salt

¼ teaspoon hot red pepper flakes

¼ teaspoon freshly ground
   pepper

Hot cooked pasta of your choice

In a food processor, place the yellow onion, carrots, celery, and salt pork. Process with on-off pulses until the mixture is finely chopped. In a stockpot, heat the olive oil and sauté the vegetable mixture until tender. Stir in the red wine and simmer 3 minutes. Stir in the tomato puree, tomato paste, salt, red pepper flakes, and pepper. Bring the mixture to a boil, reduce the heat, and simmer, partially covered, for 30 minutes. Serve over your favorite hot cooked pasta.

10 to 12 servings

Meatballs and Sauce

Meatballs

1 pound ground beef

1 pound ground veal

2 Italian sausages, broken up

1½ cups seasoned bread crumbs

1 large egg

½ cup catsup

½ cup grated Parmesan cheese

½ cup chopped parsley

¼ cup soy sauce

1½ teaspoons salt

¼ teaspoon freshly ground
   pepper

1 medium onion, finely chopped

2 carrots, finely chopped

2 celery stalks, finely chopped

3 tablespoons olive oil

Sauce

2 tablespoons olive oil

3 garlic cloves, minced

½ cup dry red wine

Two 29-ounce cans tomato puree

2 pounds spaghetti

Salt and freshly ground pepper
   to taste

For the meatballs. In a large bowl, stir together the beef, veal, sausage, bread crumbs, egg, catsup, Parmesan cheese, parsley, soy sauce, salt, and pepper. Then add half the onion, carrots, and celery. Using a small scoop or your hands, shape the mixture into 1½-inch balls. In a large skillet, heat the oil and brown the meatballs on all sides. Set aside.

For the sauce. In a large pot, heat the oil and sauté the garlic for 2 minutes. Add the remaining onion, carrots, celery, and sauté 2 minutes more. Stir in the red wine and simmer, stirring frequently, for 3 minutes. Stir in the tomato puree. Bring to a boil, then reduce the heat. Add the meatballs and simmer, partially covered, for 30 minutes.

Meanwhile, cook the spaghetti in a large pot of boiling salted water according to the package directions. Drain. Season with salt and pepper to taste. Serve the meatballs and sauce over the spaghetti.

12 to 14 servings. Recipe can be halved.

Sausage and Pork Sauce

Simmering the pork bones in the sauce gives it extra flavor.

1 medium onion, chopped
1 carrot, chopped
1 celery stalk, chopped
2 garlic cloves
2 tablespoons olive oil
4 bone-in pork loin chops
2 hot Italian sausages, broken up

½ cup dry red wine
One 6-ounce can tomato paste
2 cups canned tomato puree

Hot cooked penne
Grated Romano cheese for garnish

In a food processor, combine the onion, carrot, celery, and garlic. Cover and process until finely chopped. In a large skillet, heat the olive oil and sauté the vegetables for 5 minutes. Meanwhile, remove the pork meat from the bones, reserving the bones. Chop the meat into ½-inch cubes. Add the chopped pork, pork bones, and sausage to the skillet. Brown the meat until it is no longer pink. Stir in the wine and cook for 3 minutes. Add the tomato paste and cook for 1 minute, stirring constantly. Add 1 tomato-paste-can of water and the tomato puree. Bring to a boil, then reduce the heat. Simmer, partially covered, for 1 hour. Discard the bones. Serve over penne and sprinkle with Romano cheese.

6 to 7 servings

Pork Rib Sauce

1 rack baby back ribs

1 medium onion, quartered

1 celery stalk, quartered

1 carrot, quartered

4 garlic cloves, halved

3 tablespoons olive oil

4 medium boneless pork chops,
    cut into ½-inch cubes

8 ounces ground pork

½ cup dry red wine

Two 29-ounce cans tomato puree

1 teaspoon salt

Cut the ribs into individual pieces and set aside. In a food processor, place the onion, celery, carrot, and garlic. Cover and process until finely chopped. In a large, heavy pot, heat the oil. Add the vegetables and sauté for 3 minutes. Remove from the pan. In the same pan, brown the chops, ground pork, and ribs in batches. Drain off the excess fat. Return the vegetables and meat to the pan and pour in the red wine. Simmer 3 to 4 minutes. Stir in the tomato puree and salt. Bring the mixture to a boil, then reduce the heat. Simmer, partially covered, for 1½ hours, stirring occasionally and adding 1 to 2 cups more water if the mixture becomes too thick.

10 servings

Tomato Sauce with Prosciutto and Baby Peas

¼ *cup olive oil*

1 medium onion, finely chopped

1 carrot, finely chopped

1 celery stalk, finely chopped

6 to 8 slices prosciutto or Danish ham, finely chopped

One 29-ounce can tomato puree

Salt and freshly ground pepper to taste

¾ *cup frozen loosepack baby peas*

Hot cooked penne

In a large skillet, heat the oil and sauté the onion, carrot, celery, and prosciutto until tender, about 10 minutes. Stir in the tomatoes, salt, and pepper to taste. Bring to a boil, reduce the heat, and simmer, partially covered, for 30 minutes. Stir in the peas and cook 5 minutes more. Serve over penne.

5 to 6 servings

Tomato Sauce with Sirloin

1 cup chopped onion

1 carrot, chopped

1 celery stalk, chopped

2 garlic cloves, minced

3 tablespoons olive oil

2½ to 3 pounds sirloin steak, cut
   into ½-inch cubes

½ cup dry red wine

One 6-ounce can tomato paste

One 29-ounce can tomato puree

½ teaspoon salt

Hot cooked pasta of your choice

In a food processor, place the onion, carrot, celery, garlic, and
1 tablespoon of the olive oil. Cover and process until finely chopped. In a
large skillet, heat the remaining oil and brown the meat. Drain off the excess
fat. Stir in the wine and simmer until almost all of the liquid has evaporated,
about 2 to 3 minutes. Stir in the chopped vegetables and tomato paste.
Simmer 5 minutes, stirring frequently. Stir in 2 tomato-paste-cans of water.
Stir in the tomato puree, ½ puree-can of water, and salt. Bring to a boil,
reduce the heat, and simmer, partially covered, for 1 hour. Serve over your
favorite pasta.

8 servings

Linguine with Clam Sauce.

Clam Sauce

½ cup olive oil

4 garlic cloves, minced

¼ teaspoon hot red pepper flakes

Two 6½-ounce cans minced
    clams

1 cup chopped Italian parsley

12 Littleneck clams

½ cup water

½ cup white wine

1 garlic clove

1 pound linguine

Salt and freshly ground pepper
    to taste

In a large sauté pan over medium heat, heat the oil and sauté the garlic until golden. Add the red pepper flakes, minced clams, and parsley, and simmer for 3 minutes.

Place the whole clams, water, wine, and garlic clove in a separate pan. Bring to a simmer over high heat, lower the heat, cover, and steam the clams until they open.

Cook the linguine according to the package directions. Drain and add to the clam-and-parsley mixture. Toss well. Garnish with the whole steamed clams.

4 servings

Cristina's Pesto

4 cups fresh basil leaves

4 cups (about 1 bunch) Italian parsley sprigs

5 garlic cloves, peeled

2 cups olive oil

Salt and freshly ground pepper to taste

In a food processor, place the basil leaves, Italian parsley, and garlic. Cover and process until finely chopped. Add the oil, cover, and process until the mixture is pureed. Season with salt and pepper. Pesto can be refrigerated up to several weeks or frozen for up to 6 months.

3 cups. Recipe can be halved.

Note. Freeze pesto in ice-cube trays, then place the cubes in plastic freezer bags. Use whenever needed.

Anchovy Sauce

½ cup olive oil

5 garlic cloves, sliced

½ teaspoon hot red pepper flakes

One 2-ounce can anchovies

Chopped Italian parsley for garnish

In a small saucepan over medium heat, heat the olive oil, then add the garlic, hot pepper flakes, and anchovies. Sauté until the garlic is golden and the anchovies start to break apart.

To serve, spoon over pasta of your choice and garnish with chopped parsley.

About 1 cup sauce

Feel-good Food

Chicken Pot Pie with Cornbread Crust

Cristina's Greatest Cheeseburger

Baked Beef Ribs

Low-fat Meat Loaf

Stuffed Cabbage Rolls

Liver and Caramelized Onions

Location Sandwiches

Cottage Fries with Onions and Garlic

Split Pea Soup

Tuscan Bread Soup

Pasta Fagioli

Chicken Pot Pie with Cornbread Crust (page 223).

f Tony is feeling tired and stressed out at the office, he'll call me and say, "You know what I would really like, honey?" When he says that, I know what's coming. He wants feel-good food.

Tony is Greek, and is passionate about everything in life. Eating is right up there with his greatest pleasures. He loves all kinds of food and will eat anything, but the thing he enjoys most is basic peasant food. He thinks nothing of ordering pigs' knuckles or sucking the marrow right out of the bone of a tender hock of osso buco. I have a repertoire of feel-good foods, and Tony chooses whatever he likes. These are the dishes that mean home, warmth, and security—old-fashioned dishes that just make people happy.

One of my favorite recipes in this list is for Location Sandwiches. I call them that because I first tasted them at five o'clock in the morning while on location for a movie called The Impossible Years *that I did with David Niven in 1967. The guys on the crew were eating these great-looking sandwiches and drinking steaming cups of coffee, and I said, "That's for me!" I had one, then another, and they've been a staple in my life ever since. Now, on occasion, I use tortillas in the recipe and make breakfast burritos. Tony and I love to binge on them for a midnight treat!*

I've also included a recipe for Liver and Caramelized Onions, which is a little frightening to people but is an absolute favorite of Tony's. It tastes a lot like veal piccata. Really!

Chicken Pot Pie
with Cornbread Crust

Filling
1 tablespoon olive oil
1 tablespoon unsalted butter
1 medium onion, chopped
¼ cup all-purpose flour
2 cups chicken stock or broth
2 cups chopped cooked chicken
½ cup frozen sweet peas
½ cup chopped cooked potato
½ cup chopped cooked carrots
½ teaspoon salt

Dash of freshly ground pepper
Dash of Tabasco sauce
Cornbread crust
¾ cup yellow or white cornmeal
¾ cup all-purpose flour
1 tablespoon baking powder
1½ tablespoons sugar
½ teaspoon salt
¾ cup milk
1 large egg
2 tablespoons canola oil

Preheat the oven to 400°F. Spray a 2-quart casserole with cooking spray.

For the filling. In a large saucepan, heat the oil and butter and sauté the onion until tender but not brown. Stir in the flour until blended. Slowly stir in the stock, whisking well. Cook the mixture over medium heat until thickened and bubbly, about 2 minutes. Then cook 2 minutes more. Stir in the chicken, peas, potatoes, carrots, salt, pepper, and Tabasco and cook until the mixture is heated through. Turn into the prepared dish, spreading evenly.

For the crust. In a bowl, stir together the cornmeal, flour, baking powder, sugar, and salt. Stir in milk, egg, and oil and mix until well combined. Spoon the batter evenly over the filling. Bake until the top is golden brown, about 22 to 25 minutes. Cut into wedges to serve.

4 to 6 servings. Recipe can be doubled.

Cristina's Greatest Cheeseburger.

Cristina's Greatest Cheeseburger

The secret to a great burger is to have your butcher grind the chuck for you on the spot.

8 hamburger buns
2 pounds ground chuck
2 tablespoons olive oil

¼ cup soy sauce
8 slices American cheese
Condiments of your choice

Preheat the oven to 350°F. Wrap the hamburger buns in aluminum foil and place them in the oven for 20 minutes to warm.

Form the ground chuck into 8 thick patties and set aside.

Dip an old kitchen towel or paper towel in the olive oil and wipe the inside of a large cast-iron skillet or two smaller ones. Heat the skillet until extremely hot. Put patties into the skillet and sear over high heat for 2½ minutes on each side. Pour the soy sauce over the patties and allow to sizzle. Top each patty with a slice of cheese and cover the skillet with a lid. Allow to cook for 2 to 3 minutes more.

Assemble the burgers and top with your favorite condiments.

8 servings

Baked Beef Ribs

12 beef short ribs
1 large onion, chopped
¼ cup olive oil
½ cup dry red wine

2 teaspoons salt
**½ teaspoon freshly ground
 pepper**
1 to 2 cups water

Preheat the oven to 350°F.

In a large skillet, brown the ribs and onion in two batches in the oil until the meat is browned. Drain off the excess fat and return the meat to the skillet. Stir in the wine, salt, and pepper and cook for 5 minutes. Transfer the ribs and sauce mixture to a large baking pan and add 1 cup water. Cover and bake until the ribs are tender, about 1 to 1¼ hours. (If the liquid cooks dry, add more water, ½ cup at a time.)

4 servings

Low-fat Meat Loaf

1 cup catsup

3 pounds ground turkey

1 medium onion, finely chopped

1 carrot, finely chopped

1 celery stalk, finely chopped

1/2 cup soy sauce

1/2 large egg white

2 slices fresh white bread, torn
    into large pieces

1/2 cup packaged bread crumbs

1/2 cup grated Romano cheese

1/2 cup chopped parsley

1 teaspoon salt

1/2 teaspoon freshly ground
    pepper

Preheat the oven to 325°F. Spray two 9 x 5-inch loaf pans with cooking spray. Reserve 1/4 cup of the catsup for the top of the meat loaf.

In a large bowl, stir together the ground turkey, remaining catsup, and all remaining ingredients in the order given. Mix until well combined. Pack the turkey mixture into the prepared pans and spread the reserved catsup over the tops. Set the loaf pans on a baking tray and fill the tray with 1/4 inch of water to keep the meat loaves from drying out. Bake for 1 hour. If the tops of the meat loaves are not golden, turn on the broiler for a few minutes. Carefully drain any liquid from the pans. Let the meat loaves stand for 5 to 10 minutes before removing from the pans. Slice and serve.

12 servings

Stuffed Cabbage Rolls

Filling

2 tablespoons olive oil

2 carrots, chopped

2 celery stalks, chopped

1 medium onion, chopped

1 pound ground beef

½ pound ground veal

½ pound ground pork

3 tablespoons unsalted butter

2 tablespoons all-purpose flour

1 cup milk

1 cup cooked white rice

½ cup chopped parsley

1 teaspoon salt

¼ teaspoon freshly ground
   pepper

¼ to ½ teaspoon cayenne

1 large or 2 medium heads green
   cabbage

Sauerkraut sauce

1 tablespoon olive oil

1 medium onion, chopped

One 16-ounce jar sauerkraut
   with liquid

3½ cups of your favorite tomato
   sauce

1 tablespoon caraway seed

Preheat the oven to 325°F.

For the filling. In a large skillet, heat the oil and sauté the carrots, celery, and onion until tender but not brown. Remove and set aside. In the same pan, cook the beef, veal, and pork together until brown. Drain well and set aside. In a small saucepan, melt the butter and stir in the flour. Stir in the milk and cook and stir until the mixture thickens and bubbles, about 2 minutes. Simmer 2 minutes more. In a large bowl, stir together the cooked vegetables, drained meat, white sauce, rice, parsley, salt, pepper, and cayenne to taste. Set aside.

To prepare the cabbage leaves. Cut the core from the cabbage, but leave it whole. Immerse the cabbage head in boiling water for about 1 minute to loosen the leaves. Remove from the water and drain. Peel the leaves from the head (you'll need about 26 leaves). Place the leaves back into the boiling water and cook until limp, about 3 to 4 minutes. Drain well.

To assemble the rolls, lay each cabbage leaf on a work surface and spoon about 2 tablespoons filling into the center. Fold the sides over the filling and roll up from the short side. Place each roll seam-side down in a large greased baking pan.

For the sauerkraut sauce. In a small skillet, heat the oil and sauté the onion until tender. Stir in the sauerkraut and spoon the mixture evenly over the cabbage rolls. Top with the tomato sauce and caraway seeds. Cover with foil and bake for 50 minutes. Remove the foil and bake 10 minutes more.

12 to 13 servings. Recipe can be halved.

Liver and Caramelized Onions

½ cup plus 2 tablespoons olive oil

4 red onions, thinly sliced

Salt and freshly ground pepper to taste

½ cup all-purpose flour

Eight quarter-pound pieces calves' liver

2 garlic cloves, smashed

¼ cup cream sherry

Juice of 1 lemon

Chopped Italian parsley for garnish

To caramelize the onions, heat the ½ cup olive oil in a large sauté pan over medium heat and add the onions, tossing to coat with the oil. Season with salt and pepper. Reduce the heat to low and cook the onions until golden brown and tender, about 30 to 35 minutes.

Meanwhile, season the flour with salt and pepper. Dredge the liver in the flour and shake off any excess.

In a medium skillet over medium heat, heat the 2 tablespoons olive oil, add the garlic, and sauté briefly. Discard garlic. Sauté the liver slices 2 to 3 minutes on each side until brown. Add the sherry and lemon juice and cook for 1 minute to coat the liver with sauce.

Serve the liver with the caramelized onions and garnish with parsley.

4 servings

Location Sandwiches

2 English muffins

8 slices bacon

2 large eggs

Dash Tabasco sauce

2 slices American cheese

1 teaspoon mayonnaise

1 teaspoon Dijon mustard

1 small onion, sliced

Lettuce

Tomato slices

Cook the bacon in a medium skillet over medium heat. Remove and drain on paper towels. In the same skillet, fry the eggs. Punch a hole in the yolk so that some runs out. Sprinkle some Tabasco sauce on the eggs and place a slice of cheese on each egg. Cover the frying pan, then turn off the heat and let the cheese melt.

On one half of an English muffin spread half the mayonnaise and on the other half spread half the mustard. Now build your sandwich.

2 servings

Cottage Fries
with Onions and Garlic

4 Idaho potatoes, unpeeled, scrubbed

½ cup olive oil

6 to 8 garlic cloves, sliced

2 medium onions, thinly sliced

Cut the potatoes into ¼-inch rounds. In a large skillet over medium heat, heat the olive oil and sauté the potatoes, garlic, and onions until the potatoes are done through and golden brown, about 30 minutes.

4 servings

Split Pea Soup.

Cristina Ferrare's Family Entertaining

Split Pea Soup

If you don't see ham hocks or shanks in the pork section of your meat counter, check with your butcher.

1 pound (2 cups) dry split peas
2 tablespoons olive oil
1 medium onion, chopped
2 carrots, chopped
2 celery stalks, chopped
2 smoked ham hocks or shanks,
   or 1 ham bone

2½ quarts water
1 teaspoon salt
½ teaspoon freshly ground
   pepper
Croutons for garnish

Place the split peas in a 2-quart saucepan with enough water to cover the peas by 2 inches. Bring to a boil and boil 2 minutes. Remove from the heat, cover, and let stand for 1 hour. Drain and rinse the split peas. In a heavy pot, heat the oil and sauté the onion, carrots, and celery until tender. Stir in the ham hocks and peas. Add the water, cover, and bring to a boil. Reduce the heat and simmer, uncovered, until thick, about 2 to 2½ hours. Remove the ham hocks, let cool, and remove the meat from the bones. Chop the meat and return it to the pot. Add salt and pepper. Serve soup topped with croutons.

6 to 8 servings

Tuscan Bread Soup

1 tablespoon olive oil

6 garlic cloves, minced

⅛ to ¼ teaspoon hot red pepper flakes

Two 28-ounce cans diced tomatoes in juice

2 cups chicken stock or broth

1 teaspoon salt

¼ teaspoon freshly ground pepper

10 slices day-old bread, torn into bite-size pieces

Fresh basil leaves and shredded Parmesan cheese for garnish

In a heavy pot, heat the oil and sauté the garlic and red pepper flakes over medium-high heat for 2 minutes. Stir in the tomatoes with their juice, stock, salt, and pepper. Bring to a boil, reduce the heat, and simmer, uncovered, for 20 minutes. To serve, sprinkle some bread pieces into each soup bowl. Pour the soup over the bread and garnish with basil leaves and Parmesan cheese.

5 to 6 servings

Pasta Fagioli

1 pound dry navy beans
1 medium yellow onion, chopped
4 ounces salt pork, chopped
½ cup tomato puree
4 cups chicken stock or broth
1 to 2 cups water
1 teaspoon salt

¼ teaspoon freshly ground
  pepper
8 ounces mini pasta shells
Grated Parmesan cheese and
  chopped fresh basil for
  garnish

Rinse the beans and place them in a large saucepan with enough water to cover by 2 inches. Bring the mixture to a boil and boil 2 minutes. Remove from the heat, cover, and let stand 1 hour. Drain and rinse the beans. Drain again. In a heavy pot, sauté the onion with the salt pork for 5 minutes. Stir in the beans, tomato puree, chicken stock, 1 cup of the water, salt, and pepper. Bring to a boil, reduce the heat, and simmer, partially covered, until the beans are tender, about 2 hours. (Add another cup of water, if necessary, during cooking.) While the beans are cooking, cook the pasta in a large pot of boiling salted water according to the package directions. Drain and set aside.

In a blender or food processor, puree half the bean mixture. Return to the pot with the cooked beans and stir in the pasta. Garnish each serving with Parmesan cheese and basil.

5 to 6 servings

Recipe Index

*I*cing, cream cheese, carrot cake with, 168
Italian bread salad (panzanella), 89
Italian peas, 50
Italian sausage
    and peppers, 28
    and pork sauce, 212

*K*ick-butt chili, 30
Killer brownies, 117

*L*amb, marinated leg of, 48
Lasagna, deep-dish, 152
Last-minute biscuits, 104
Lemon-walnut vinaigrette, Bibb lettuce
        with, 175
Lettuce, endive, with walnut-gorgonzola
        dressing, 41
Liver and caramelized onions, 230
Lobster, in seafood salad, 141
Location sandwiches, 231
Low-fat meat loaf, 227

*M*acaroni and cheese casserole, 124
Mango sorbet with fresh raspberry
        sauce, 188
Marinade, Cristina's famous, 96
Marinara, 209
Marinated beef, 27
Marinated leg of lamb, 48
Marinated turkey with chive gravy, 97
Mascarpone, homemade, tiramisù with,
    42

Mashed potatoes, 100
Meatballs
    chicken, pastina con brodo with, 20
    and sauce, 211
    veggie-, farfalle pasta with, 114
Meat loaf, low-fat, 227
Mexican wedding balls, 160
Mixed baby greens with crumbled blue
        cheese, 144
Mousse
    chocolate, cake, 22
    raspberry, frozen, 64
Mushroom, wild, risotto, 130
Mustard. See also Dijon (mustard)
    -glazed salmon, 139
Mustard greens, sautéed, 154

*N*ony's ravioli, 204

*O*ctopus salad, 142
Onions
    cottage fries with garlic and, 231
    liver and caramelized, 230
Orange-walnut cranberry sauce, 103
Orzo salad, 49
Osso buco, 18
Oven-baked tortilla chips with homemade
        salsa and guacamole, 183
Oven-roasted chicken with honey Dijon
        glaze, 11